# Banking Law and Financial Regulation in Pakistan

This book offers an analysis of the contemporary significance of the practice of Lender of Last Resort (LOLR) in Pakistan. Aiming to identify deficiencies in current financial system legislation, the book details the role of LOLR and its essential presence in establishing a resilient banking and financial system.

Beginning with an assessment of the emergence of Central Banks as domestic financial regulators, the book draws from the principles of Walter Bagehot and Henry Thornton for LOLR rescue operations. Examining the International Monetary Fund's (IMF) role as an international lender of last resort and scrutinising its rescue efforts, the book uses case studies of the Central Banks in the United Kingdom and the United States to suggest reforms for Pakistan's system. It explores the causes of financial crises and evaluates the factors that have made LOLR an integral part of Central Banks' responsibilities. It compares LOLR operations in the cases of AIG and Lehman Brothers in the United States and Northern Rock in the United Kingdom, comparing these two cases in Pakistan to pinpoint key gaps in the State Bank of Pakistan's LOLR operations. Furthermore, it discusses the Basel Accord I, II, and III: the key international regulations for the banking sector.

The book will be of interest to scholars and students in the field of financial and banking law.

**Muhammad Hassan Idrees** is a dynamic legal attorney with an enthusiasm for learning contemporary legal issues. He has a profound interest in international banking and financial laws, alternative dispute resolution, civil and criminal litigation, corporate and taxation laws. He has completed a B.A.LL.B (Hons) from the University of the Punjab, Lahore, Pakistan; LL.M in International Business and Corporate Law with Distinction from the University of Bedfordshire, UK; and a PhD in Law, from Canterbury Christ Church University, UK. Hassan Idrees is also a member of the Honourable Society of Lincoln's Inn. Currently, he is working as a legal consultant for the Federal Board of Revenue, Pakistan, and a barrister/advocate in the High Courts of Pakistan.

# Banking Law and Financial Regulation in Pakistan

## The Role of Lender of Last Resort

**Dr. Muhammad Hassan Idrees**

Routledge
Taylor & Francis Group
LONDON AND NEW YORK

First published 2024
by Routledge
4 Park Square, Milton Park, Abingdon, Oxon OX14 4RN

and by Routledge
605 Third Avenue, New York, NY 10158

*Routledge is an imprint of the Taylor & Francis Group, an informa business*



*British Library Cataloguing-in-Publication Data*
A catalogue record for this book is available from the British Library

ISBN: 978-1-032-74130-7 (hbk)
ISBN: 978-1-032-76504-4 (pbk)
ISBN: 978-1-003-47876-8 (ebk)

DOI: 10.4324/9781003478768

Typeset in Times New Roman
by Apex CoVantage, LLC

# Contents

# Preface

This book provides insight into the contemporary significance of the doctrine of Lender of Last Resort (LOLR). Also, it attempts to identify lacunas in the legislation with regards to the financial system – which is a primary obstacle in the way of achieving a stabilised/prosperous financial system in Pakistan. Appraisal of the role of LOLR is provided besides the explication of its inevitable presence to establish an invulnerable banking and financial system. The emergence of the Central Banks (CB) as a domestic financial regulator is evaluated along with the principles of Walter Bagehot and Henry Thornton for the rescue operations of LOLR. It further argues about the emergence of the International Monetary Funds (IMF) as an international lender of last resort and examines its rescue operations.

In order to deter financial crisis, the Central Bank (CB) plays the role of LOLR by taking necessary steps. The operations of LOLR of the Central Banks of the United Kingdom and the United States of America are used as examples to propose reforms for the system of Pakistan. Furthermore, the book examines the causes of financial crises and evaluates the factors that paved the way for LOLR to become an integral part of the responsibilities of CBs. The LOLR operations in the cases of AIG and Lehman Brothers from the United States of America and Northern Rocks from the United Kingdom are evaluated through a comparative study of the case of KASB from Pakistan to determine the pivotal gaps in the LOLR operation of the State Bank of Pakistan. Basel Accord I, II and III, which is an international regulation for the banking sector, is also discussed.

In order to provide reform proposals in legislation, current laws which regulate LOLR and their limitations are examined. There are currently two types of banking systems operating in Pakistan, which are commercial and Islamic banks. The latter operates interest-free banking, which could limit the effectiveness of the LOLR mechanism. Notwithstanding, this book mainly addresses the commercial banking sector of Pakistan. A reform proposal is recommended for the financial system of Pakistan according to the lessons learned from the illustrations of the UK and the USA. This book concludes the comprehensive discussion of LOLR by providing a critical analysis of the recommended reform proposals to determine their viability for the financial system of Pakistan.

# Acknowledgements

I would like to dedicate my book to my wonderful parents, Mr. & Mrs. CHAUDHARY MUHAMMAD IDREES, whose unyielding support backed me throughout my educational career. Also, I want to thank a special friend who bears with me through the thick and thin of my life.

# 1 Introduction

Lender of last resort is one of the fundamental duties of the Central Bank. In the modern financial system, it is the responsibility of the CB to maintain stability in the system and strengthen financial institutions against financial crises. The main aim of this chapter in this book is to provide a comprehensive rationale behind selecting this topic for research. It provides a brief argument on the contemporary significance of the topic of research. Furthermore, two figures are also used in this chapter to demonstrate that there are loopholes that will be addressed in this book.

## 1.1 Rationale

Lending liquidity to financial institutions that are in need of liquidity has been in practice for over 200 years.[1] From the outset, many policymakers and even Central Banks were against the existence of a lender of last resort (LOLR) and believed that its presence will lead to a fragile domestic banking system.[2] The rationale behind the existence of LOLR was nothing more than imparting liquidity to the financial institutions facing a shortage of liquidity, thereby deterring a financial crisis. Furthermore, the survival of the banking industry rests upon the trust of its creditors.[3] Therefore, a financial panic among the creditors can increase the demand for liquidity and create a situation in which it becomes impossible for the banks to deter a financial crisis.[4]

The presence of LOLR assures the creditors that, in the time of financial need, the CB would intervene and rescue the financial institutions by imparting

1 Robert E. Keleher and Thomas M. Humphery, "The Lender of Last Resort: A Historical Perspective" (1984) *Cato Journal*, Vol. 4, No. 1, Page No. 275.

2 Paul Kosmetatos, *The 1772 73 British Credit Crisis* (Springer, 2018), Page No. 191, ISBN: 978-3-319-70907-9.

3 Robert E. Keleher and Thomas M. Humphery, "The Lender of Last Resort: A Historical Perspective" (1984) *Cato Journal*, Vol. 4, No. 1, Page No. 275.

4 Paul Kosmetatos, *The 1772 73 British Credit Crisis* (Springer, 2018), Page No. 191, ISBN: 978-3-319-70907-9.

DOI: 10.4324/9781003478768-1

liquidity. This provides stability in the financial institutions by allowing them to overcome a liquidity shortage/shortage of liquidity. The principle set by the early academics that the Central Banks should only provide liquidity support to the financial institutions which are capable of providing collateral and this facility of liquidity should also be set on high-interest rates.[5]

However, there are certain discretionary powers attached to the function of LOLR which the Bank of England (BOE) has used in the best interest of its financial system during financial crises.[6] It lent liquidity to the financial institutions even on a lower interest rate and has denied operating as a LOLR in certain cases.[7] For example, the BOE adopted an uncommon approach and nationalised the Bank of Northern Rocks instead of imparting liquidity to it. The decisions of the BOE were quite helpful in protecting financial institutions from a collapse during the financial crisis of 2007–2008 and enhanced the functions of LOLR in the UK.[8]

Similarly, in the United States, the Federal Reserve played an imperative role in strengthening its financial institutions during the financial crisis of 2007–2008.[9] The liquidity support was provided to the financial institutions which were capable of providing adequate collateral.[10] The Federal Reserve rescued AIG and refused to extend liquidity support to Lehman Brothers because the bank was not complying with the rules set by the Federal Reserve.[11]

The State Bank of Pakistan (SBP), which was established on the model of BOE,[12] has, however, struggled to maintain stability in the financial system of Pakistan. The powers of the SBP to act as a LOLR are also based on the principle of Walter Bagehot, which provides that it should only lend to the financial institutions that can provide sufficient collateral. Furthermore, frequent

5 See Chapter two (Walter Baghot and Honery Thornton).

6 Gayane Oganesyan, "The Changed Role of LOLR: Crisis Responses of Federal Reserves, European CB and Bank of England" (2013) Institute for International Political Economy Berlin 19/2013, Accessed: March 30, 2018.

7 Mike Anson, David Bholat, Miao Kang and Ryland Thomas, "The Bank of England as Lender of Last Resort: New Historical Evidence from Daily Transactional Data" (2007) The Bank of England 691/2017, Accessed: April 10, 2018.

8 Robert E. Keleher and Thomas M. Humphery, "The Lender of Last Resort: A Historical Perspective" (1984) *Cato Journal*, Vol. 4, No. 1, Page No. 275.

9 Stanley Fischer, "The Lender of Last Resort Function in the United States" (2016) *International Finance*, Vol. 2, Page No. 239–60.

10 Paul Kosmetatos, *The 1772–73 British Credit Crisis* (Springer, 2018), Page No. 191, ISBN: 978-3-319-70907-9.

11 Hansjörg Herr, Sina Rüdiger and Jennifer Pédussel Wu, "The Federal Reserve as Lender of Last Resort During the Subprime Crisis – Successful Stabilisation Without Structural Changes" (2016) Berlin School of Economics, Accessed: April 01, 2020.

12 C. A. E. Goodhart, "Myths About Lender of Last Resort" (1999) *International Finance*, Vol. 2, Page No. 339–60.

political interference and continuous engagement of the SBP in LOLR's operations have created uncertainty in the financial system of Pakistan.[13]

The International Monetary Fund (IMF) played the role of international LOLR for Pakistan because a continuous engagement of the SBP in rescuing the national and financial institutions made it difficult for the SBP to survive without the intervention of an ILOLR. The LOLR operation of the SBP, in the case of KASB bank, is one of the most recent cases which is examined and discussed in detail in Chapter 6 of this study. However, the involvement of the IMF could not bring stability to the financial system of Pakistan.[14]

To this end, the study aims to evaluate the doctrine of LOLR and appraise the financial regulatory framework in Pakistan in order to determine whether the reform is essential in relation to the function of LOLR. Furthermore, the study evaluates the practical application of the doctrine of LOLR in the UK and the USA in order to draw lessons from its operations and provide recommendations beneficial to Pakistan.

It is important to understand that the rationale behind the existence of LOLR is not only to lend liquidity in tough conditions but to maintain the stability in the financial system. An apprehension among the investors about the stability of the financial system rapidly increases the demand for liquidity, which is the most annihilating factor for a system, ultimately resulting in its collapse. Nonetheless, the assurance of the CB that it will play the role of LOLR and address the issue eliminates the panic which decreases the demand for liquidity.[15] Usually, to address the issue of liquidity, the financial institutions sell their illiquid assets and handle the issue, whereas the absence of a LOLR raises the demand and compels the financial institutions to sell their assets swiftly. A rapid sale of assets mostly deteriorates their value and makes the situation more difficult to handle for financial institutions.[16] Imparting liquidity is not the only mandate the LOLR has; the CBs can purchase the illiquid assets of the financial institutions to provide liquidity.

To further illustrate the research problem, two tentative charts are used to show the operational system of the financial system in the UK and Pakistan.

Figure 1.1 explains the financial system of the UK. It further illustrates that the Central Bank injects liquidity into the financial system which includes banks. Depositors also invest their money in the financial system and play an imperative role in maintaining stability in the economic system of a country.

13 Muhammad Farooq Arby, "State Bank of Pakistan: Evolution, Functions and Organization" (2009) MPRA Paper No. 13614, Accessed: June 10, 2018.

14 Ibid.

15 Paul Tucker, "The LOLR and Modern Central Banking: Principles and Reconstruction" (2014) Bank for International Settlement, Page No. 10.

16 Marc Dobler, Simon Gray, Diarmuid Murphy and Bozena Radzewicz-Bak, "The LOLR Function After the Global Financial Crisis" (2016) IMF Working Paper No. 16/10, ISBN: 9781498355995/1018-5941, Accessed: May 17, 2017.

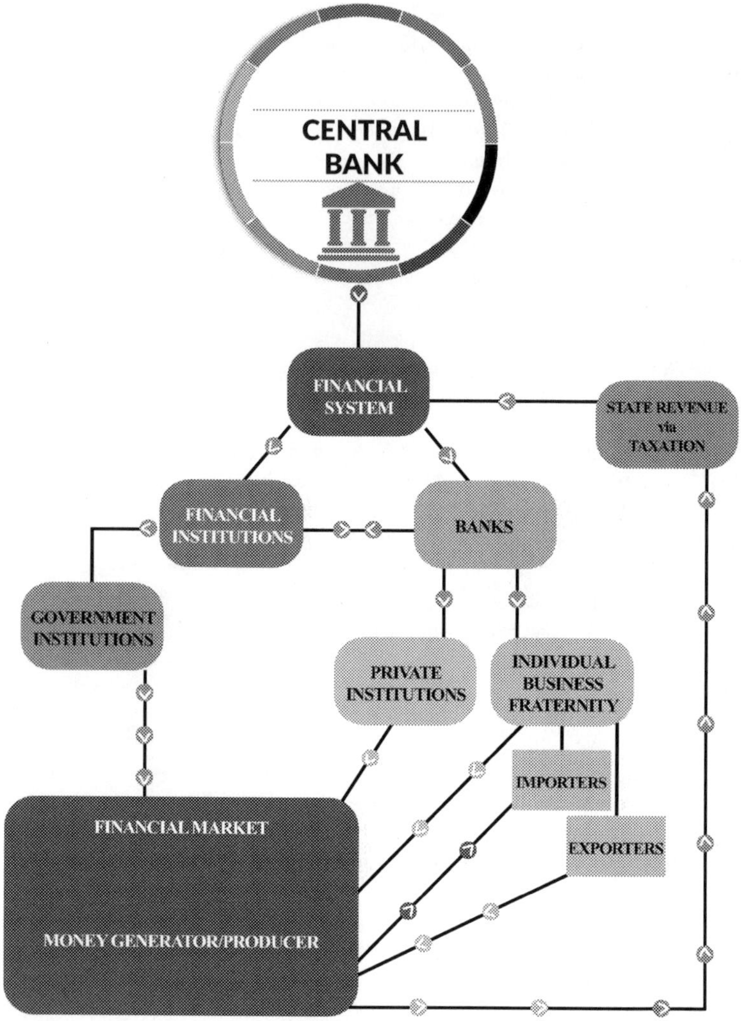


*Figure 1.1* Tentative Figure of Financial System of a Developed Country (UK, USA).

The main acumen behind having an efficient system of LOLR is not to inject liquidity during financial unrest but to ensure the trust of the depositors in the system. If a financial system loses the trust of its depositors, it enhances the demand for liquidity and makes it difficult to prevent a recession. Thereby, the trust of the depositors is required to maintain stability in the financial system of a country. This is why, in developed countries – i.e., the UK and USA – financial regulators pay heed to ensure the trust of the depositors in the financial system. Banks lend liquidity to companies and business groups for commercial ventures. Financial bodies put their money into the financial market and earn more money through their business activities. The State helps them by providing the facilities, such as law and policy, to carry out their business. The State, on the other hand, recovers money via direct and indirect taxation. However, if the financial institution is faced with any liquidity crisis, the Central Bank intervenes and imparts liquidity, which strengthens these financial institutions to overcome the liquidity crisis.[17] The ability of the Central Bank to inject liquidity during any financial unrest prevents the financial situation from further escalation. Thus, the strength of a financial system rests on the trust of the creditors in the system.

Figure 1.2 explains the financial system of Pakistan and its problems. The figures portray the current financial problems and explain how an effective regulatory framework will be able to address these issues. Furthermore, Figure 1.2 depicts the reasons why SBP is incessantly involved in the rescue operations of financial institutions. It further explains the problems of the financial system in Pakistan. The logic behind the operation of LOLR is to rescue the financial system against the financial crisis and bring stability. The SBP has lost money through this process, and this is partly caused by the gaps in the regulatory framework (see Chapter 5), and hence, the need for regulatory reform. The law regulating LOLR is found in section 17 of the State Bank of Pakistan Act, 1956. It states that:

> 17G. Lender of last resort. – Where the circumstances so warrant and a scheduled bank approaches the Bank for the financial facility to improve its liquidity and where the bank in the opinion of the Bank, is solvent and can provide adequate collateral to support the financial facility, the Bank may provide the financial facility, in accordance with the regulations made by the Bank in relation thereto.[18]

Based on Figure 1.2, the Central Bank lends liquidity to financial institutions and banks. Financial institutions that include government institutions utilise this money for business purposes. Banks and businesses invest money into the financial market, and a large amount goes out for the payment of imported goods and money lending. In order to create a balance in maintaining the flow of the liquidity, the State imposes more direct and indirect taxes, which curtail the margin of profits. The figure further explains that, in such situations, the

17 Paul Tucker, "The LOLR and Modern Central Banking: Principles and Reconstruction" (2014) Bank for International Settlement, Page No. 10.

18 The State Bank of Pakistan Act, 1956, Section 17G.

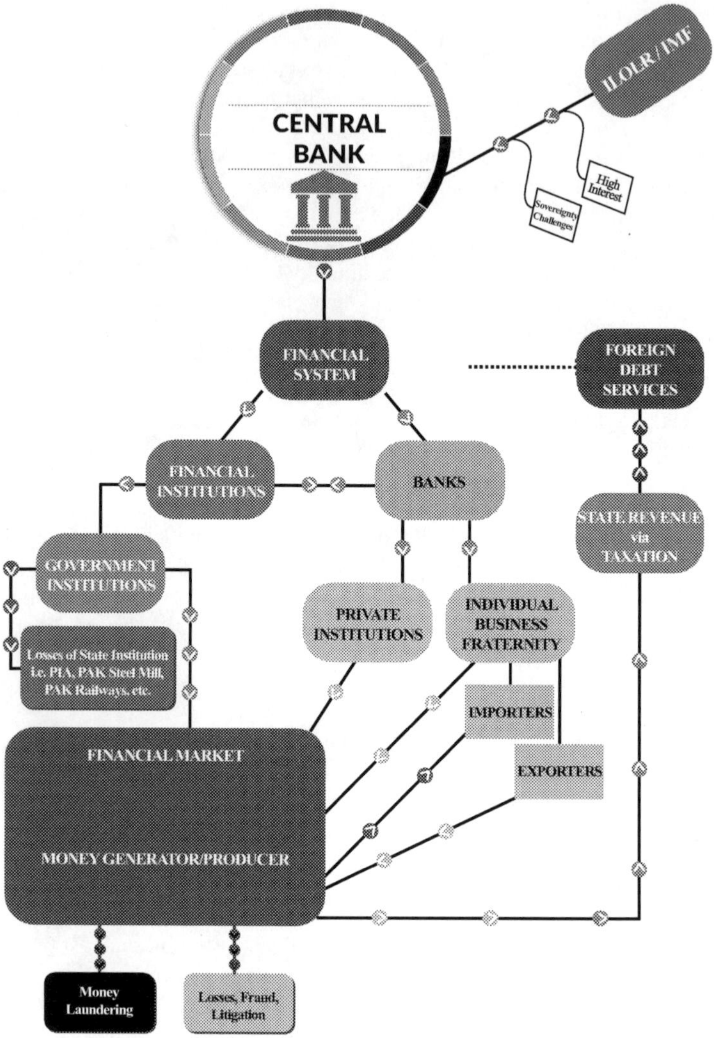


*Figure 1.2* Tentative Figure of Financial System of Pakistan.

Central Bank can request the intervention of the ILOLR/IMF to maintain the flow of liquidity.[19] This raises several questions regarding the LOLR and its operation in Pakistan.

19 Edwin M. Truman, "The IMF as an International Lender of Last Resort" (October 12, 2010) Peterson Institute for International Economics, Accessed: February 04, 2018.

This study aims to examine the regulatory and practical application of the Lender of Last Resort doctrine in Pakistan. In doing so, it will appraise the financial systems in the UK and USA and draw lessons that will eventually be used for my recommendation for Pakistan. The previously mentioned figures are used to identify the problems in the financial system of Pakistan in the context of LOLR.

# 2 Conceptual Underpinning of the Lender of Last Resort

The main purpose of this chapter in this research is to explain the role of LOLR in detail at the domestic and international levels. The former chapter of this book provided the significance and reasons for this research. However, this chapter starts by providing a brief introduction to the legal system of Pakistan and its contemporary financial issues. Furthermore, it provides a comprehensive argument on the evolution of the doctrine of LOLR. This chapter also talks about the emergence of the IMF as an international LOLR. This chapter concludes by arguing the potential moral hazard problems pertaining to the role of LOLR.

## 2.1 Conceptual Underpinning

Pakistan gained its independence from Britain in 1947, and the country's legal system derives its roots from English common law. Pakistan is the fifth largest country in the world.[1] The State Bank of Pakistan was established on the model of the Bank of England on 1 July 1948 by the founding father of Pakistan, Muhammad Ali Jinnah.[2] Aside from the commercial banking system, Pakistan also has an Islamic banking system.[3] The State Bank of Pakistan has played the role of lender of last resort (LOLR) for its financial system several times since its establishment. The country has been rescued by the International Monetary Fund (IMF) over 18 times.[4] This study aims to identify the gaps in the regulatory framework of Pakistan to propose a suitable

1 World Population Review, <https://worldpopulationreview.com/>, Accessed: November 10, 2019.

2 A Journey Towards Professional Excellence, <http://www.sbp.org.pk/70/his.asp>, Accessed: February 10, 2020.

3 Muhammad Mahmood Shah Khan, Bushra Shafiq and Farrukh Ijaz, "An Empirical Analysis of Banking Sector in Pakistan: Islamic Versus Conventional Banks" (2017) *International Journal of Islamic Economics and Finance Studies*, Vol. 3, No. 1, Page No. 61.

4 Sara Cheema, "The IMF: Pakistan's History and Future with the LOLR", *Eurasia Review* (2017), Accessed: April 21, 2018.

DOI: 10.4324/9781003478768-2

framework for LOLR, using the financial systems of the UK and USA to draw lessons for the financial system in Pakistan.

LOLR has been defined as an operation that injects liquidity into the financial market to avoid a recession.[5] Prior to the present times, its main function was to lend liquidity on demand. Thus, all-natural and legal persons who possessed sufficient liquidity and were capable of lending were considered eligible to play the role of LOLR.[6] Today, the CB holds the resources of the State and is generally empowered to release new notes; hence, Sir Frances Baring (1797) argued that the CBs are the main operators of the role of LOLR for the financial system.[7] The impartation of liquidity by private institutions to each other does not cover the entire meaning of LOLR. Private institutions are not bound to adhere to the goals of LOLR because they lend liquidity for business or personal motives. Nonetheless, the CB is under an obligation to support the growth of the financial system and protect it from any financial crisis.[8]

In a financial system, it is unsurprising for a financial institution to face liquidity problems and be unable to address the issue by using its resources. Therefore, CBs intervene and lend liquidity to financial institutions. The operation of CBs is not to protect an individual institution, but it works for the protection of an entire system.[9] Many economists have argued that injecting liquidity into the financial system is not a solution to deter a financial crisis; rather, it leads to depletion of resources. The current role of LOLR does not prevent financial institutions from imparting liquidity to each other.[10]

However, CBs cannot lend liquidity without following certain principles. If the CBs provide complete assurance that they will back all financial institutions in times of crisis, it could create moral hazard problems. Thus, to curtail moral hazard problems, it is necessary to implement a financial policy regarding LOLR, which can only be done by CBs.[11] Like domestic financial institutions, it is also possible that a CB starts enduring liquidity problems; therefore, the IMF is playing the role of international LOLR. Notwithstanding, there are several principles regarding the operation of LOLR which explain why only

5 Paul Kosmetatos, *The 1772 73 British Credit Crisis* (Springer, 2018), Page No. 191, ISBN: 978-3-319-70907-9.

6 Paul Tucker, "The LOLR and Modern Central Banking: Principles and Reconstruction" (2014) Bank for International Settlement, Page No. 10.

7 Robert E. Keleher and Thomas M. Humphery, "The Lender of Last Resort: A Historical Perspective" (1984) *Cato Journal*, Vol. 4, No. 1, Page No. 275.

8 Paul Tucker, "The LOLR and Modern Central Banking: Principles and Reconstruction" (2014) Bank for International Settlement, Page No. 10.

9 Michael D. Bordo, "Rules for a Lender of Last Resort: An Historical Perspective" (2014) *Journal of Economic Dynamics and Control*, Vol. 49, Page No. 126.

10 Paul Kosmetatos, *The 1772 73 British Credit Crisis* (Springer, 2018), Page No. 191, ISBN: 978-3-319-70907-9.

11 Mikko Niskanen, "Lender of Last Resort and the Moral Hazard Problem" (2002) Bank of Finland No. 17/2002, Accessed: August 10, 2017.

CBs are capable of being regarded as a LOLR for the system. These principles are extensively examined in the next section.

## 2.2 Evolution of LOLR Domestically

The role of LOLR has been through an intense evolutionary process. In 1797, the term "dernier resort" was used for the CBs by Sir Francis Baring in his book *Observations on the Establishment of the Bank of England.*[12] It was not only the CB that could play this role, but the financial institutions were also capable of lending liquidity for business or personal interests.[13] Imparting liquidity to the financial institutions facing a liquidity crisis was considered as being the sole role of LOLR. This move was criticised and did not get the attention of the policymakers. Therefore, any institution or private individual who would lend liquidity was considered as the LOLR, which was justifiable in those times.[14] Afterward, Henry Thornton (1802) argued that moral hazard problems are inseparable from LOLR.[15] Additionally, he argued that private financial institutions are obliged to safeguard the interest of their customers. Therefore, lending liquidity for other financial institutions against interest rates is a business activity for them. However, CBs owe wider obligations; hence, they must ensure the trust of the investors in the economic system, which prevents the financial institutions from aggregated demand for liquidity.[16]

Walter Bagehot (1873) took the ideas of Henry Thornton regarding LOLR and, further, argued that the CB will only play this role when the existence of the entire economic system comes under threat. The CB comes under the obligation to strengthen the financial institutions against a crisis through the role of LOLR.[17] Bagehot extended the sphere of LOLR merely from lending liquidity to the protector of the system by arguing that CB can take any decision to earn the trust of depositors instead of merely imparting liquidity.[18] Furthermore, he argued that CB should follow certain principles while acting as LOLR because it cannot let any financial institution waste public money.

12 See Chapter two (Sir Francis Baring).

13 Robert E. Keleher and Thomas M. Humphery, "The Lender of Last Resort: A Historical Perspective" (1984) *Cato Journal*, Vol. 4, No. 1, Page No. 275.

14 David Grad, Perry Mehrling and Daniel H. Neilson, "The Evolution of Last-Resort Operations in the Global Credit Crisis" (March 2011) <https://ssrn.com/abstract=2232348>, Accessed: May 20, 2017.

15 C. A. E. Goodhart, "Myths About Lender of Last Resort" (1999) *International Finance*, Vol. 2, Page No. 339–60.

16 Michael D. Bordo, "Rules for a Lender of Last Resort: An Historical Perspective" (2014) *Journal of Economic Dynamics and Control*, Vol. 49, Page No. 126.

17 David Laidler, "Central Bank as the LOLR-Trendy or Passe" (2004) University of Western Ontario, Economic Policy Research Institute 20048, Accessed: May 20, 2017.

18 Thomas M. Humphrey, "LOLR: The Concept in History" (1989) *FRB Richmond Economic Review*, Vol. 75, No. 2, Page No. 8.

He suggested that CB should lend freely and make its policy clear and state the grounds for supporting LOLR. Bagehot also tried to address the moral hazard problems which Henry Thornton had highlighted and argued that, if these problems remain unaddressed, LOLR will be unable to protect the system against a crisis.[19]

According to Bagehot, the CB should charge a high-interest rate on its liquidity support.[20] He was also of the opinion that CBs should also lend only against worthy collaterals. Nonetheless, there are no principles to determine the solvency of the institutions, and it is still a discretionary power of the CB.[21] However, there are certain cases when CBs were coerced to protect some financial institutions because their fall would subsequently affect the entire economic system. This, in turn, defeated the idea of demanding good collateral from financial institutions before lending liquidity. All the arguments by these philosophers revolved around lending liquidity or preventive steps to overcome the financial crisis.

However, the role of LOLR is still emerging in developing countries, and many countries are reluctant to authorise their CBs to play this role because of moral hazard problems. As stated earlier, one of the research aims is to examine the nature of LOLR in Pakistan and propose a regulatory framework for it.

## 2.3 The Emergence of the IMF as an International LOLR

In the domestic financial systems, the support of liquidity to financial institutions has been occurring even before the existence of CBs. In the United Kingdom, it was Sir Francis Baring (1797) who argued, while explaining the characteristics of CBs, that it is a LOLR for domestic financial institutions.[22] In the United States, before the establishment of Federal Reserves (1913), the financial institutions were playing this role individually.[23] The banks were mainly playing this role, and it was a business activity for them to lend liquidity and charge an interest rate to earn money.

Different countries played this role based on their interest or political affiliations and rescued the economic system of other countries by providing

19 David Laidler, "Central Bank as the LOLR-Trendy or Passe" (2004) University of Western Ontario, Economic Policy Research Institute 20048, Accessed: May 20, 2017.

20 See Chapter two (Walter Baghot).

21 Thomas M. Humphrey, "LOLR: The Concept in History" (1989) *FRB Richmond Economic Review*, Vol. 75, No. 2, Page No. 8.

22 Denis O. Brien, "The LOLR Concept in Britain" (2003) *History of Political Economic*, Vol. 35, No. 1, Page No. 1–19.

23 Jerome H. Powell, "America's Central Bank: The History and Structure of the Federal Reserves" (2017) A Speech at the West Virginia University College of Business and Economics Distinguished Speaker Series, Accessed: April 20, 2018.

liquidity. The countries, on mutual understandings and mainly due to political relations, lend liquidity to each other. There are several cases where one country lent liquidity to another country without charging any interest. However, this was happening purely on the basis of diplomatic relations, but the emergence of global financial systems and the nature of crises raised the need for an international LOLR.[24] The Bank of England and the Banque de France played this role in the early nineteenth century to stabilise the world economic system.[25] However, domestic LOLR paved the way for the organisation of an institution that is capable enough to play this role with all of its essential characteristics. Currently, the International Monetary Fund (IMF) is playing this role. The IMF also faces several operational challenges – i.e., it cannot lend liquidity to personal relations.[26] However, it can play the role of a consultant.[27] The countries who are playing the role of LOLR for each other were not following any principles to lend liquidity and made their rules for it.[28] IMF is not seen to ask for worthy collaterals to impart liquidity like the CBs, but it asks for a viable plan to return the money.[29] To curtail moral hazard problems, the IMF also charges high-interest rates.[30] Notwithstanding, the role of the IMF as a LOLR in the last two decades has become controversial, which is evident from the way it deals with developing countries. Instead of assisting the borrowing countries, the IMF is seen trying to apply its influence.[31]

The insight behind the establishment of the IMF was not to make them an international LOLR.[32] CBs have several powers to act as LOLR, and they can intervene at any stage to protect the financial institutions without their permission. However, the IMF cannot intervene unless the government of the State asks for assistance. Before the Latin American Crisis (1982),

24 Stanley Fischer, "On the Need for an International LOLR" (1999) *The Journal of Economic Perspectives*, Vol. 13, No. 4, Page No. 85.

25 Mark Traugott, "The Mid-Nineteenth-Century Crisis in France and England" (1983) *Theory and Society*, Vol. 12, No. 4, Page No. 455.

26 Camila Villard Duran, "The International Lender of Last Resort for Emerging Countries: A Bilateral Currency Swap?" (2015) The Global Economic Governance Programme University of Oxford, Page No. 1–33.

27 Jean-Pierre Landau, "International LOLR: Some Thoughts for 21st Century" (2014) Bank for International Settlement No. 79, Page No. 119.

28 Forrest Capie, "Can There Be an International Lender of Last Resort?" (2002) *International Finance, Wiley Blackwell*, Vol. 1, No. 2, Page No. 311.

29 Jean-Pierre Landau, "International LOLR: Some Thoughts for 21st Century" (2014) Bank for International Settlement No. 79, Page No. 119.

30 Camila Villard Duran, "The International Lender of Last Resort for Emerging Countries: A Bilateral Currency Swap?" (2015) The Global Economic Governance Programme University of Oxford, Page No. 1–33.

31 Sara Cheema, "The IMF: Pakistan's History and Future with the LOLR", *Eurasia Review* (June 19, 2017), Accessed: April 21, 2018.

32 Stanley Fischer, "On the Need for an International Lender of Last Resort" (1999) *Journal of Economic Perspectives*, Vol. 13, No. 4, Page No. 85–104.

the IMF was lending liquidity for the short term, but it started lending for a longer period afterward.[33] The rationale behind the establishment of the IMF was to curtail poverty in the world.[34] Thus, in 1999, Poverty Reduction and Growth Facility (PRGF) eliminated the role of Enhanced Structural Adjustment Facility (ESAF), which was used to provide long-term liquidity on an appropriate interest rate to the poor countries.[35] IMF reformed its functions and started lending liquidity to the countries which were facing financial crises. It was significant for the global economic system to have a neutral institution that could play the role of ILOLR for all countries.[36]

In this modern era, international laws and institutions have become indispensable elements for the survival of the global world. The global financial crisis coerced economists to realise that, in case of the collapse of an international economic system, the endurance of the domestic system is nothing more than an illusion. The framework offered by Walter Bagehot in the nineteenth century, in which the operations of LOLR were proposed against good collaterals, was basically for the domestic role of LOLR.[37] It became inevitable at the domestic level because of numerous reasons. Similarly, the existence of an international LOLR also becomes inevitable because a CB can also face a liquidity crisis as well as require the support of ILOLR. However, the importance of the role of LOLR paved the way for the organisation of a proper institution that is capable enough to play this role with all of its essential characteristics. Therefore, currently, the International Monetary Fund (IMF) is playing this role. The IMF also faces several operational challenges, and it cannot lend liquidity to personal relations. It cannot give financial policy for the country which is taking assistance from it; however, it can play the role of a consultant.[38]

33 Curzio Giannini, "The IMF and LOLR Function: An External View" (1999) *Finance & Development*, Vol. 36, No. 3, Page No. 1.

34 Giancarlo Corsetti, Bernardo Guimaraes and Nouriel Roubini, "International Lending of Last Resort and Moral Hazard: A Model of IMF's Catalytic Finance" (2006) *Journal of Monetary Economics*, Vol. 53, No. 3, Page No. 441.

35 International Monetary Fund (1999a) for a description of the mandate in Poverty Reduction and Growth Facility. For a discussion of the evolution of the IMF's activities over time, Boughten (1998), Krueger (1998), Vasquez (1999), Overseas Development Council (2000) and International Financial Institution Advisory Commission (2000), Accessed: March 15, 2018. Sourabh Kumar. *World Affairs: The Journal of International Issues*. Vol. 15, No. 1 (SPRING (JAN-MARCH) 2011), pp. 60–71 (12 pages). Published By: Kapur Surya Foundation.

36 Camila Villard Duran, "The International Lender of Last Resort for Emerging Countries: A Bilateral Currency Swap?" (2015) The Global Economic Governance Programme University of Oxford, Page No. 1–33.

37 Curzio Giannini, "The IMF and LOLR Function: An External View" (1999) *Finance & Development*, Vol. 36, No. 3, Page No. 1.

38 Jean-Pierre Landau, "International LOLR: Some Thoughts for 21st Century" (2014) Bank for International Settlement No. 79, Page No. 119.

## 2.4 Contemporary Significance of LOLR

In the modern economic system, the role of LOLR has become a vital part of the functions of CBs. It was not a part of major policy debates before the financial crisis of 2007–08. It was argued that the assurance of having an institution that will eventually provide liquidity to handle the crisis allows the financial institutions to take a plunge in the risky act without bothering about the consequences.[39] Its presence eliminates the role of investors to put an eye on the business activities and compels the administrators not to involve in such ventures. It will allow the financial system to ruin the public money injected into it by the CB while acting as LOLR. However, it holds several benefits and strengthens financial institutions against any crisis. In this modern era when multinational companies are working in financial markets and they are using various currencies for their businesses, there are many reasons which can put even a solvent institution into a situation where it would face liquidity problems. Mere liquidity issues can escalate the demand for liquidity because of the apprehensions of the crisis. Thus, the presence of a LOLR can handle the situation by lending liquidity.[40] It is important to understand that the rationale behind the existence of LOLR is not merely to lend liquidity in tough conditions but to maintain the stability of the financial system.

A dread among investors rapidly increases the demand for liquidity, which is the most annihilating factor for a system to collapse. Nonetheless, the assurance of the CB that it will play the role of LOLR and address the issue eliminates the panic, which decreases the demand for liquidity.[41] Usually, to address the issue of liquidity, financial institutions sell their illiquid assets and handle the issue, whereas the absence of a LOLR raises the demand and compels the financial institutions to sell their assets swiftly. A rapid sale of assets mostly deteriorates their value and makes the situation more difficult for financial institutions to handle.[42] Imparting liquidity is not the only mandate the LOLR has; the CBs can purchase the illiquid assets of the financial institutions to provide liquidity. The presence of LOLR is inevitable for modern financial systems. Notwithstanding, there are several moral hazard problems pertaining to this role that needs to be addressed.[43] Moral hazard problems

39 Paul Tucker, "The LOLR and Modern Central Banking: Principles and Reconstruction" (2014) Bank for International Settlement, Page No. 10.

40 Kathryn Judge, "The Role of a Modern Lender of Last Resort" (2016) *Columbia Law Review*, Vol. 116, Page No. 843.

41 Paul Tucker, "The LOLR and Modern Central Banking: Principles and Reconstruction" (2014) Bank for International Settlement, Page No. 10.

42 Marc Dobler, Simon Gray, Diarmuid Murphy and Bozena Radzewicz-Bak, "The LOLR Function After the Global Financial Crisis" (2016) IMF Working Paper No. 16/10, ISBN: 9781498355995/1018-5941, Accessed: May 17, 2017.

43 Mikko Niskanen, "Lender of Last Resort and the Moral Hazard Problem" (2002) Bank of Finland 17/2002, Accessed: August 10, 2017.

are extensively described in Chapter 2 of this book. The benefits of having a LOLR can be seen in the recent financial crisis; however, it is important to implement the principles while playing this role. There was criticism of this role because of the apprehensions of wasting the public money, but strong regulations are capable of addressing the moral hazards. Thus, in contemporary financial issues, LOLR is regarded as a strong tool to address them.[44]

In the modern economic system where the CBs are playing the role of LOLR and strengthening the financial institutions against recession, it is also possible that CB itself starts facing a situation that is difficult to handle.[45] Although the CB of a State has the power to emit new notes, issuing new notes can cause inflation. However, in such a situation where the CB is facing liquidity problems, there must be an international LOLR that can rescue the economy of that country. Contemporarily, IMF is playing the role of an ILOLR. In the globalised economy, the collapse of a domestic economy can harm other systems; hence, the ILOLR is as important as a domestic LOLR.[46]

## 2.5 Moral Hazards Pertaining to LOLR

The impartation of liquidity support to the financial institutions experiencing the shortage of liquidity will be futile if the inseparable moral hazard problems are not properly addressed.[47] The moral hazard problems are the main reasons for curtailing the benefits of LOLR; therefore, it is befitting to identify the reasons which are causing these problems and address them.[48] For instance, the purchase of illiquid assets prevents the depreciation of the assets. However, the assistance of the CBs through purchasing illiquid assets does not stop the financial institutions from investing in risky ventures. Frequent purchases of such assets can create a situation where the position of the CB to handle the crisis will be compromised.[49] Any sort of assistance in

44 Marc Dobler, Simon Gray, Diarmuid Murphy and Bozena Radzewicz-Bak, "The LOLR Function After the Global Financial Crisis" (2016) IMF Working Paper No. 16/10, ISBN: 9781498355995/1018-5941, Accessed: May 17, 2017.

45 Frederic S. Mishkin, "The International Lender of Last Resort: What are the Issues?" (2000) Graduate School of Business, Columbia University and National Bureau of Economic Research, Page No. 1.

46 Giancarlo Corsetti, Bernardo Guimaraes and Nouriel Roubini, "International Lending of Last Resort and Moral Hazard: A Model of IMF's Catalytic Finance" (2006) *Journal of Monetary Economics*, Vol. 53, No. 3, Page No. 441.

47 Kathryn Judge, "The Role of a Modern Lender of Last Resort" (2016) *Columbia Law Review*, Vol. 116, Page No. 843.

48 Marc Dobler, Simon Gray, Diarmuid Murphy and Bozena Radzewicz-Bak, "The LOLR Function After the Global Financial Crisis" (2016) IMF Working Paper No. 16/10, ISBN: 9781498355995/1018-5941, Accessed: May 17, 2017.

49 Vittorio Corbo, "Financial Stability in a Crisis: What Is the Role of the Central Bank?" (2010) BIS Paper No. 51, Accessed: April 04, 2018.

the operations of LOLR without addressing the issue of moral hazard problems will cause inefficiency and expedite the dependency of the financial system on the CB, which will create a frailer economic system.[50] To curb the moral hazard problems, CBs must stipulate that no financial institution will be eligible to seek liquidity support if it cannot provide worthy collateral. CBs should penalise these financial institutions by charging a high rate of interest on their support.[51] Bagehot also emphasised that a frequent involvement of the CBs in rescue operations will make it difficult for the CBs to maintain stability. Thus, the backing of the LOLR in the form of impartation of liquidity of illiquid assets should only be offered to illiquid but solvent institutions.[52]

Notwithstanding, there were no parameters offered by Bagehot and Thornton to evaluate if the financial institutions are just illiquid or insolvent. The example of the Bank of Bulgaria is important. The Bank of Bulgaria applied Bagehot's principles and rescued the solvent institution and refused to extend its support to a bank that was insolvent in their view.[53] This approach was used to minimise the effects of moral hazard problems. However, it was later established that the evaluation of the CB was wrong in determining the solvency of the institutions, as it rescued an insolvent financial institution instead of rescuing a solvent bank.[54]

A domestic system works with the alliance of all of the financial institutions in the country, and their existence is mutually dependent. The collapse of a financial system can escalate panic among investors and create financial unrest. Similarly, in the modern global economic system, the collapse of the economy of a country can create an international financial crisis like that of 2007–2008.[55] International LOLR has played its role in the recent financial crisis and strengthened the global economic system against the financial crisis. However, it also faces moral hazard problems like domestic LOLR.[56] The IMF, in the current era, has emerged as an international LOLR and has lent

50 Avinash Persaud, "How Can Central Banks Avoid Another Financial Crisis?" (August 21, 2014) World Economic Forum, Accessed: April 04, 2018.

51 Mikko Niskanen, "Lender of Last Resort and the Moral Hazard Problem" (2002) Bank of Finland 17/2002, Accessed: August 10, 2017.

52 Paul Tucker, "The LOLR and Modern Central Banking: Principles and Reconstruction" (2014) Bank for International Settlement, Page No. 10.

53 Michael Berlemann, Kalin Hristov and Nikolay Nenovsky, "Lending of Last Resort, Moral Hazard and Twin Crises Lessons from the Bulgarian Financial Crisis 1996/1997 (2002) William Davidson Institute Working Paper No. 464, Accessed: February 10, 2018.

54 Ibid.

55 Paul Kosmetatos, *The 1772–73 British Credit Crisis* (Springer, 2018), Page No. 191, ISBN: 978-3-319-70907-9.

56 Robert E. Keleher and Thomas M. Humphery, "The Lender of Last Resort: A Historical Perspective" (1984) *Cato Journal*, Vol. 4, No. 1, Page No. 275.

liquidity to more than 50 countries.[57] The dealing of IMF is with the CBs of the States; that is why it cannot lend liquidity directly to the financial institutions. At the international level, when a CB realises that it is incondensable to avoid the financial crisis with its resources, it decides to seek assistance from the IMF.[58]

57 Jean-Pierre Landau, "International LOLR: Some Thoughts for 21st Century" (2014) Bank for International Settlement No. 79, Page No. 119.

58 Camila Villard Duran, "The International Lender of Last Resort for Emerging Countries: A Bilateral Currency Swap?" (2015) The Global Economic Governance Programme University of Oxford, Page No. 1–33.

# 3 Banking Regime of Pakistan, Basel Accord and LOLR

This chapter consists of the literature related to the banking industry of Pakistan and explains the diversity of the banking sector in the country. The concerned chapter is divided into five parts; the first part of this chapter explicates the significance of the banking system in the modern economic systems and its contribution to the growth of financial systems around the globe. It explores the progression of the banking industry in Pakistan and analyses various approaches that have been used to develop the banking sector. Additionally, this part appraises the policies of nationalisation and privatisation for the financial institutions and examines their impacts on the banking sector in detail. It further explains the basic difference between the operating systems of conventional and Islamic banks. The second part of this chapter unfolds the effects of financial crises on the systems and also unveils the reasons which cause financial crises.

The third part of this chapter critically examines the current laws which regulate the banking sector of Pakistan. Additionally, it explains the key features of the Banking Companies Ordinance, 1962 (LVII of 1962). The fourth part of this chapter describes the inception of the Basel Accord and extensively explains the reasons behind the failure of banking regulations, which became the reason for crises. Furthermore, it explains the regulations of Basel Accord I and analyses its limitations. It also explicates the features of Basel II and III. Finally, it explains the implementation of Basel III in Pakistan. The final part of this chapter surmises the role of LOLR and argues the legitimacy of LOLR in Pakistan by explaining the laws relating to it. Moreover, it brings into light the problems which Pakistan is facing in establishing a LOLR for Islamic banks.

## 3.1 Banking Regime of Pakistan, Basel Accord and LOLR

In a modern financial system, the vigorous contribution of banks to the growth of Gross Domestic Productivity (GDP) has made the banks an integral part of the system. A strong banking system is indispensable to deter the contemporary

DOI: 10.4324/9781003478768-3

challenges being faced by the financial systems. The first bank in the world was established in 1407 in the Republic of Genoa (The Bank of St George). Banks obtain funds from depositors and lend to financial institutions (borrowers), which allows them to enhance their business activities.[1] Banks ensure the security of the funds of the depositors, who have surplus money but do not wish to get engaged in business activities and provide these funds to individuals or business corporations who are ready to take risks through their business activities. The banks perform the role of a guarantor by providing funds to financial institutions that contribute towards an increase in business activities. The absence of banking facilities in an economic system will dramatically shrink business ventures, which will result in a diminution of GDP.[2]

The banking industry is not merely an essential part of the financial system; it is also embedded in our lives. The collapse of the banking industry can cause a recession, which will affect all the inhabitants of the State, no matter whether they are engaged with banks in any way or not. The stability of the banking industry relies on the trust of the depositors; nonetheless, if the public loses its confidence in the banking system, this will increase the demand for liquidity, which will cause a financial crisis. Hence, an efficient banking system is the mainstay of the sustainability of the financial system.[3]

Trust in the banking sector allows people to overcome the anxiety of the financial crisis and maintain stability in the financial system. Financial institutions do not merely get debts or loans from the banks; they are also using banks for their transactions, which is a transparent and convenient mode of business.

The Banking Sector of Pakistan operates through the Banking Companies Ordinance 1962 (LVII of 1962), and the State Bank of Pakistan (SBP) plays the role of surveillant, empowered by the SBP Act 1956 (SBPA). The banking history of Pakistan is as old as the history of Pakistan. The SBP was established on 1 July 1948 and holds all the resources of the State; it is empowered to regulate the banking sector. The core functions of Central Banks (CBs) are to conduct monetary policies and implement them.[4] The CBs supervise and regulate depository institutions. They also maintain stability in the financial

1 Ibish Mazreku, Fisnik Morina and Sami Mazreku, "The Role of the Banking System on the Financing of the Businesses and the Determinants of the Lending Level on the SMEs in Kosova" (August 07, 2016) SSRN, Accessed: October 05, 2018.

2 Neslihan Dincbas, Tomasz Kamil Michalski and Evren Ors, "Banking Integration and Growth: Role of Banks' Previous Industry Exposure" (2017) HEC Paris Research Paper No. FIN-2015/1096, Page No. 21.

3 Kelvin Mkwawa, "Importance of Banking Industry", *The Citizen* (May 03, 2018), Accessed: October 05, 2018.

4 Heidi Mandanis Schooner, "Central Banks' Role in Bank Supervision in the United States and United Kingdom" (January 2003) *Brooklyn International Law Journal*, Vol. 28, Accessed October 06, 2018.

system of the State by taking all possible measures. It is the responsibility of a CB to ensure the trust of the depositors in the system.

The CB of the State is the only institution that can emit new notes when needed and implement financial policies. Every CB of the State plays the role of Lender of Last Resort (LOLR) for its financial institutions when they face a liquidity crisis.[5] Similarly, the SBP utilises all its resources to maintain financial stability in Pakistan. The banking industry of Pakistan is more diverse than that of many other countries because it has two different banking systems: one is a conventional banking system that works according to the conventional rule of interest-based banking, and the other banking system is known as Islamic banking, which works as interest-free banking.[6] Before appraising the banking regime of Pakistan, it is important to elucidate the conception of these conventional and Islamic banking systems.

The conventional banks' operations are based on the rules set by the Board of Directors of such banks. They can establish their rule of business but cannot cross the borderline set by the SBP. The conventional banks have a fixed interest rate by which they receive money from the depositors and lend to the borrowers. Interest is the main source of income for conventional banks because they offer less interest rates to the depositors and charge a higher interest rate from the debtors. They do not bear any risk and shift it to the debtors. The core responsibility of the banking industry is to play the role of intermediary between the depositors and debtors.[7]

On the other hand, the Islamic banking sector claims to follow the injunctions of Sharia laws. Therefore, Islamic banks do not operate on fixed rates for depositors and debtors. The main source of earnings for this sector is service charges, consultancy, and share in profits. They jointly share the risk with the lender, the debtor, and the bank. Islamic banks get shares in the business of the debtors and then, based on that share, they offer a percentage to the lenders. The Islamic banking industry has been emerging swiftly over the last decade and a half. Many economists argue that the Islamic banking industry could perform better if there were a separate legal framework to address its operational challenges.[8]

5 Ibish Mazreku, Fisnik Morina and Sami Mazreku, "The Role of the Banking System on the Financing of the Businesses and the Determinants of the Lending Level on the SMEs in Kosova" (August 07, 2016) SSRN, Accessed October 05, 2018.

6 Muhammad Mahmood Shah Khan, Bushra Shafiq and Farrukh Ijaz, "An Empirical Analysis of Banking Sector in Pakistan: Islamic Versus Conventional Banks" (2017) *International Journal of Islamic Economics and Finance Studies*, Vol. 3, No. 1, Page No. 110.

7 Ashfaq Ahmad, Muhammad Imran Malik and Asad Afzal Humayoun, "Banking Developments in Pakistan: A Journey from Conventional to Islamic Banking" (2010) *European Journal of Social Sciences*, Vol. 17, No. 1.

8 Muhammad Mahmood Shah Khan, Bushra Shafiq and Farrukh Ijaz, "An Empirical Analysis of Banking Sector in Pakistan: Islamic Versus Conventional Banks" (2017) *International Journal of Islamic Economics and Finance Studies*, Vol. 3, No. 1.

## 3.2 Progression of the Banking Sector in Pakistan

Every country strives to establish a sound and prosperous economic system by utilising all the resources of the State. Each economic system has its dynamics based on religious and social values. Thus, it is not possible to import a financial system from a developed country to govern the system.[9] The history of the banking sector of Pakistan starts from 14 August 1947, when it gained independence from British rule. The formation of the State Bank of Pakistan in 1948 officially regulated the banking industry. An economic system can bring prosperity and establish a strong financial system if it is framed according to the needs of the financial market. Pakistan, therefore, formatted its CB, which is mandated to make a financial system that can address the challenges of its economy. Pakistan's banking sector has gone through a long and intense process of evolution. It started with the conventional banking system but now has an Islamic banking system as well.[10] An uninterrupted interaction of the financial institutions to attain financial objects of having a sound economic system is inevitable, which can only be possible by judiciously utilising all the natural, human, and financial resources. The banking sector is deemed to be the most efficient and reliable means to manage financial resources across the globe.[11]

Initially, the financial system of Pakistan suffered a lot due to the absence of an efficient banking system. Nonetheless, its banking system has immensely emerged and is considered a sophisticated system now.

However, it is still going through the process of evolution and enduring technological and legislative challenges.[12] Religion has a profound relationship in every act of Pakistan because it is created on the ideology of Islam. The conventional banking sector faced serious troubles because it works based on interest (Riba), which is strictly prohibited according to the principles of Islam. Therefore, the Council of Islamic Ideology (CII) was established in 1956 to obliterate all interest-based financial activities, especially from the banking sector, and is still a part of the current constitution of Pakistan (1973).[13] The CII consulted numerous economists to propose an alternative

9 Ashfaq Ahmad, Muhammad Imran Malik and Asad Afzal Humayoun, "Banking Developments in Pakistan: A Journey from Conventional to Islamic Banking" (2010) *European Journal of Social Sciences*, Vol. 17, No. 1, Page No. 1.

10 Ahsin Shahid, Hibba Saeed and Muhammad Ali Tirmizi, "Economic Development and Banking Sector Growth in Pakistan" (2015) *Journal of Sustainable Finance & Investment*, Vol. 5, No. 3, Page No. 245.

11 Justin Baer, "History: Banks Are at the Heart of Capitalism", *Financial Times*, November 17, 2010, Accessed: October 07, 2018.

12 Ashfaq Ahmad, Muhammad Imran Malik and Asad Afzal Humayoun, "Banking Developments in Pakistan: A Journey from Conventional to Islamic Banking" (2010) *European Journal of Social Sciences*, Vol. 17, No. 1, Page No. 11.

13 Article 28, of the Constitutions of Pakistan 1956, Article 2A, 31, 37, 38F & 227 of the Constitution of Pakistan 1973.

financial structure for the banking industry of Pakistan. Additionally, the supreme court of Pakistan also ordered the erosion of interest (Riba) from the economic system until 30 June 30 1992, which was also a major setback for the conventional banking industry in Pakistan. Finally, after a long effort, Pakistan managed to establish an Islamic banking system in 2002, which is claimed to be a non-interest banking system but still not acknowledged concurrently by all religious entities.[14]

### *3.2.1 Nationalisation of Banking Sector*

In the first phase, the SBP encouraged the private sector to invest in the banking industry and established several private commercial banks. However, the unsatisfactory growth of the financial system urged the government to take unprecedented steps that could make a sound economic system. The government of Pakistan decided to nationalise all the existing 14 commercial banks.[15] The Pakistan Banking Council (PBC) was formatted for the first time to monitor the operations of these nationalised banks and the powers of SBP to regulate the financial institutions were marginalised. The rationale behind this decision was to provide maximum funds to the public industries and surge the income of the public sector. The PBC has framed a new policy and merged small banks into the banks and established five big nationalised banks from 14 commercial banks.[16] The Bank of Bahawalpur was merged into the National Bank of Pakistan. The Premier Bank Limited and Sarhad Bank Limited were merged in Muslim Commercial Bank Limited. Pak Bank Limited was merged with Allied Bank Limited. Commerce Bank Limited was merged in United Bank Limited, and Standard Bank Limited was merged in Habib Bank Limited.[17]

This nationalisation policy was aimed to discourage hoarding and distribute the wealth equally among the inhabitants of the states. It worked well for the economic system of Pakistan, and due to massive changes, the banking sector showed good growth in their profits. However, it worked well only for a short period and created equivocal financial challenges. Due to the absence of healthy competition from the private sector and lack of professionalism,

14 Dr. Hafiz Muhammad Zubair and Nadeem Ghafoor Chaudhry, "Islamic Banking in Pakistan: A Critical Review" (2014) *International Journal of Humanities and Social Science*, Vol. 4, No. 2, Page No. 377.

15 Muhammad Abrar Zahoor, "A Critical Appraisal of the Economic Reforms Under Zulfikar Ali Bhutto: An Assessment" (2010) <https://www.academia.edu/28879263/A_Critical_Appraisal_of_the_Economic_Reforms_under_Zulfikar_Ali_Bhutto_An_Assessment>, Accessed: October 07, 2018.

16 Mubashir Hasan, *The Nationalization Policy of 70's in Pakistan's Economy in the 80's: Structure and Prospects* (Press Institute of Pakistan, 1988), Page No. 255.

17 Amna Khalabat, "History of Banking in Pakistan – Of Humble Origin and Vast Potential", *The Express Tribune* (November 04, 2011), Accessed: October 15, 2018.

all the nationalised banks showed poor performance. It also discouraged private investment, and especially, a dramatic decrease in foreign investment was evident.[18] The decision of nationalisation proved to be a disaster due to the political involvement in the 1980s and 1990s. Lending decisions were politically influenced and were not commercially motivated. Thus, billions of rupees were looted from the treasury of Pakistan due to inefficient regulations and the absence of a good command and control system.[19]

### *3.2.2 Privatisation of Banking Sector*

Due to the failure of the nationalisation policy and massive loss, the government of Pakistan in the 1990s decided to privatise the banking and financial industries, which were nationalised in Bhutto's era. In that era, not only the banks but other financial institutions were also privatised to attract private and foreign investment. Hence, Muslim Commercial Bank Limited (MCB) in 1991, Allied Bank Limited in 1993, United Bank Limited in 2002, and Habib Bank Limited in 2003 were privatised consequently.[20] Initially, the privatisation policy worked well in the banking industry, and many commercial banks started their operations in Pakistan. It was also able to invite private and foreign investment in the banking sector; therefore, many foreign banks also initiated their work in Pakistan. Competition between private and public entities resulted in good services and an increase in the growth of this sector. However, lack of transparency in the process of privatisation and bad economic conditions miserably failed this policy to show any economic growth for the long term. Surprisingly, the improvement of the banking sector after privatisation in a decade was lesser than the growth it had achieved after the implementation of the policy of nationalisation.[21]

After a bad performance of the privatisation policies, transformational reforms were carried out. The original powers of the SBP to regulate financial institutions were reinstated by amending the Banking Companies Ordinance 1962 and the State Bank of Pakistan Act 1956. Lending from the banking sector was limited to big financial institutions or influential individuals; however, it was expanded and offered to microeconomic entities and common customers. So far, these reforms are working well, especially for the banking sector

18 Sulman Badshah, "Impact of Nationalization on Pakistan's Economic Development", *Pakistan Economy* (2017), Accessed: October 07, 2018.

19 Kazim Alam, "Bhutto's Economic Policies Were Disastrous for Pakistan", *The Express Tribune* (June 30, 2016), Accessed: October 07, 2018.

20 Dr Munawwar Kartio, Prof Muhammad Ishaque Bajoi and Prof Dr Ambreen Zaib Khaskelly, "Privatization of Banking Sector in Pakistan: A Case Study of MCB Bank Limited" (2017) *International Journal of Management & Information Technology*, Vol. 12, No. 1, Page No. 11.

21 Muhammad Shoaib, "Impact of Privatization on Banking Sector Performance of Pakistan" (SSRN Electronic Journal, February 2012), Accessed: October 07, 2018.

of Pakistan, and as a result, by the year 2010, there were more than 25 domestic private banks and six foreign banks which were operating in the country.[22] All these private commercial banks are now playing a positive role in the growth of GDP and motivating domestic and foreign investors to invest in the banking and financial industry of Pakistan. However, all these banks are still working on a fixed interest rate (Riba), which is still facing strong criticism from religious scholars and many economists.

### *3.2.3 Conventional Banks*

Pakistan did not have a CB at the time of its inception, and therefore, Habib Bank, established in 1941, served as a CB to fulfil this gap. The role of the banking industry was limited in the financial system of Pakistan due to the lack of essential resources. However, the establishment of SBP in 1948 played a vital role to develop commercial banks and encouraged them to enhance the financial capacity of the newly created State. SBP was mandated to make the banking industry flourish; hence, Allied Bank, Habib Bank and National Bank were supported by the SBP to start their operation.[23] Uncertainty in the political and economic condition always adversely affects the banking industry; that is why, initially, the banking industry was badly damaged due to the unstable political and financial condition of Pakistan.

The Reserve Bank of India (RBI) was working as the CB in the subcontinent till December 1947. However, it was not helping the financial system of Pakistan; instead, it played a negative role. On the serious reservations of the government of Pakistan, the British government divided the RBI on the proportion of 30/70. Pakistan got 30 percent from the division of RBI in May 1948 and immediately established its CB known as SBP.[24] In November 1949, National Bank of Pakistan has established in east Pakistan.

Nonetheless, the banking industry could not contribute to the financial system because of not having professionals in this field. The SBP was empowered through the State Bank of Pakistan Act, 1956, to allow private investors to establish commercial banks and financial institutions. However, lack of experience and corruption in public sectors became the main hurdle in the growth of this industry during the decades of 1950 and 1960.[25] Many radical changes and amendments in the laws relating to the banking and financial

22 Amna Khalabat, "History of Banking in Pakistan – Of Humble Origin and Vast Potential", *The Express Tribune* (November 04, 2011), Accessed: October 15, 2018.

23 Ibid.

24 Ashfaq Ahmad, Muhammad Imran Malik and Asad Afzal Humayoun, "Banking Developments in Pakistan: A Journey from Conventional to Islamic Banking" (2010) *European Journal of Social Sciences*, Vol. 17, No. 1, Page No. 35.

25 Ahsin Shahid, Hibba Saeed and Muhammad Ali Tirmizi, "Economic Development and Banking Sector Growth in Pakistan" (2015) *Journal of Sustainable Finance & Investment*, Vol. 5, No. 3, Page No. 235.

system of Pakistan worked well and established a relatively sound system than the one working before.[26]

### *3.2.4 The Inception of Islamic Banking in Pakistan*

The Islamic banking system does not merely exist in the sermons of religious scholars or the virtual world. It does not only operate within the financial system of Pakistan but also in many Muslim and non-Muslim countries.[27] The history of Islamic banking is not as old as conventional banking. Islamic banks do not offer or charge interest to their depositors and investors; hence, it is also known as interest-free banking. In Egypt, the very first Islamic bank, Mit Ghamr Social Bank, was established in 1963. Initially, the financial activity of this bank was limited. It collected funds from depositors and offered loans to the agricultural industry only. In 1973, the Organization of Islamic Conference (OIC) backed the concept of Islamic banking. In 1975, a foundation for Islamic Development Banking was created.[28]

After recognition of Islamic banking by the OIC, the idea disseminated around the world, especially in Muslim states where interest-free Islamic banks were established: the Philippine Amanah Bank in 1973, the Dubai Islamic Bank in 1975, the Faisal Islamic Bank of Sudan in 1977, the Bahrain Islamic Bank in 1979 and the Meezan Islamic Bank of Pakistan in 2002.[29] In 1983, Malaysia passed the Islamic Banking Act to merge all its conventional banks into Islamic banks and obliterate all interest-based banking.[30]

Between 1979 and 1992, several serious efforts were made by the Government of Pakistan to establish an interest-free financial system. In 1979, many interest-free financial institutions were established in Pakistan; for example, the National Investment Trust, the Investment Corporation of Pakistan and the House Building Finance Corporation.[31] In December 2001, the SBP officially

26 Amna Khalabat, "History of Banking in Pakistan – Of Humble Origin and Vast Potential", *The Express Tribune* (November 04, 2011), Accessed: October 15, 2018.

27 Dr Hafiz Muhammad Zubair and Nadeem Ghafoor Chaudhry, "Islamic Banking in Pakistan: A Critical Review" (2014) *International Journal of Humanities and Social Science*, Vol. 4, No. 2.

28 Dr Rukhsana Kalim, Afia Mushtaq and Noman Arshed, "Islamic Banking and Economic Growth: Case of Pakistan" (2016) *Islamic Banking and Finance Review*, Vol. 3, No. 1, Page No. 14–28.

29 Ashfaq Ahmad, Muhammad Imran Malik and Asad Afzal Humayoun, "Banking Developments in Pakistan: A Journey from Conventional to Islamic Banking" (2010) *European Journal of Social Sciences*, Vol. 17, No. 1.

30 N. Ahmad and S. Haron, "Perceptions of Malaysian Corporate Customers Towards Islamic Banking Products and Services" (2002) *International Journal of Islamic Financial Services*, Vol. 3, No. 4, Page No. 13–29.

31 Ashfaq Ahmad, Muhammad Imran Malik and Asad Afzal Humayoun, "Banking Developments in Pakistan: A Journey from Conventional to Islamic Banking" (2010) *European Journal of Social Sciences*, Vol. 17, No. 1.

explicated the criteria for establishing an Islamic bank in the private sector. In January 2002, the Al Meezan Investment Bank was able to satisfy the SBP that it complied with the principles of establishing an Islamic bank and got a license. It started its operations as the first Islamic bank of Pakistan under the name of Meezan Islamic Bank on 20 March 2002.[32]

The banking system is regarded as an integral part of any financial system and plays a vital role in economic growth.

## 3.3 Current Status of the Banking Sector of Pakistan

The journey of the banking sector of Pakistan is now subtended over seven decades, and it has emerged remarkably. However, the goal of establishing an efficient banking system that can address contemporary financial challenges is yet to be achieved. Although an imported financial system cannot address the issue of a system because each system has its compulsion, a comparative study can help to identify the lacunas in the existing system, and many lessons can also be learned.[33] Banks play a vital role in the economic development of a country, but an uncertain and deteriorating economic system makes the banking sector vulnerable because banking sectors survive only if the depositors keep their trust in the system. The banking sector of Pakistan is now improving because the local and foreign depositors are investing in this sector.

Now, due to a healthy competition between conventional and Islamic banks, the banking sector is providing good services, and to engage more customers, they are extending their loan services to the common man.[34] The banks were reluctant to offer their loan services to small business entities and private persons in the past. Only big enterprises could avail the facility of loan or it was offered based on nepotism. To attract more customers, the banks are using different methods and branchless banking has also been introduced in Pakistan – e.g., Tameer Bank, Easypaisa and UBL Omni.[35]

The competitive environment has increased awareness in the customers and a bank can only remain its customer if he is satisfied with the quality of services provided by that bank. Islamic banks are working within the limits of Shariah laws, but still, they are continuously expanding their loan facilities to various forms of business while remaining within the limitations of

32 Ibid.

33 Ahsin Shahid, Hibba Saeed and Muhammad Ali Tirmizi, "Economic Development and Banking Sector Growth in Pakistan" (2015) *Journal of Sustainable Finance & Investment*, Vol. 5, No. 3, Accessed: October 07, 2018.

34 Ashfaq Ahmad, Muhammad Imran Malik and Asad Afzal Humayoun, "Banking Developments in Pakistan: A Journey from Conventional to Islamic Banking" (2010) *European Journal of Social Sciences*, Vol. 17, No. 1, Page No. 11.

35 Amna Khalabat, "History of Banking in Pakistan – Of Humble Origin and Vast Potential", *The Express Tribune* (November 04, 2011), Accessed: October 15, 2018.

Shariah laws. Due to the competition, conventional banks are also offering several debt services, which are increasing the financial activities in the country. Islamic banks have started a new scheme (Qarz-e-Hasana 1991), in which they offer no interest and benefits to the depositors and then lend credits on an interest-free basis. However, it was observed that, due to an inefficient legal framework, these credits were only offered based on personal relations.[36] The profitability in the banking sector is directly proportional to the services which banks are offering to their customers. Islamic banks are showing swift progression because they are offering better services, as compared to conventional banks.[37] Finally, financial liberalisation can be detrimental to the system in the absence of strong regulation. Although the private sector holds much of the assets of the banking sector, the SBP must remain autonomous to regulate the banking sector of Pakistan.

## 3.4 Legal Framework to Regulate the Banking Sector of Pakistan

The history of the banking industry of Pakistan is as old as the history of the country. State Bank of Pakistan was established in July 1948 and mandated to establish a prosperous financial system. If a country is blessed with several resources but its laws are full of lacunas, it cannot survive for a long time. Pakistan's banking industry has gone through an intense process of evolution, and many different financial approaches were used to make a strong system. The Banking Companies Ordinance 1962 (LVII of 1962) regulates the banks and financial institutions of Pakistan. The salient features of these ordinances are:

Section 5 of the Banking Companies Ordinance, 1962 (LVII of 1962) explicates the key terms which are used to govern the banking industry.

- Securities are key elements of the banking industry, and this section explains approved securities which can be used in this business, in which a trustee can invest in accordance with section 20 of the Trust Act, 1882, and it will also include everything as approved securities which the federal government will declare in the official Gazette.[38]
- It further explains the term "Banking", which means accepting the money from the depositors to lend or invest. Additionally, it imposes an obligation

36 Ashfaq Ahmad, "An Overview of the Operations/Products Offered by Islamic Banks in Pakistan" (ResearchGate, June 2011), Accessed: October 20, 2018.

37 Dr. Hafiz Muhammad Zubair and Nadeem Ghafoor Chaudhry, "Islamic Banking in Pakistan: A Critical Review" (2014) *International Journal of Humanities and Social Science*, Vol. 4, No. 2, Page No. 15.

38 The Banking Companies Ordinance, 1962 (LVII of 1962), Section 5 (a)(i)(ii).

that the depositors' money will be repayable on demand and withdrawable by cheques or other means.[39]

- "Banking Company" denotes any company that will be considered as a banking company that is carrying out its business that falls under the definition of banking explained in this law. If such a company is incorporated in Pakistan, this law will apply to all of its branches and subsidiaries, even if they are working outside Pakistan. However, no company will be considered as a banking company merely on the ground if that company accepts deposits from the public to finance its business and does not fully comply with the definition of banking.[40]
- "Branch" or "Branch office" means any place where the deposits are received, cheques can be cashed and money lent from there will be recognised as a branch office of a banking company, no matter if called by pay or sub-pay office or any other name.[41]
- "Creditor" includes legal and natural persons who have surplus money to deposit in the banks for the participation in profit and loss.[42]
- "Company" means any company which is incorporated in accordance with the Companies Ordinance 1984 (XL VII of 1984). It also includes a foreign bank company carrying out its banking business in Pakistan which is being licensed by the State Bank of Pakistan.[43]
- "Debtor" includes a person, financial institution or banking company that obtains finances as defined in the Banking Tribunals Ordinance, 1984.[44]
- "Demand liabilities" means the liabilities of the financial or banking companies which must be met on demand.[45]
- "Foreign banking company" is a company which is not incorporated in Pakistan. However, it is having a branch or branches and carrying out banking business in Pakistan after obtaining a license from the State Bank of Pakistan.[46]
- "Loan" means advances, credit or finance as described in the Banking Tribunals Ordinance, 1984.[47]
- "Secured loan or advance" means a loan or advance which is offered against good collaterals having the same market value as of the loan and the loans and advance which is based on bad securities are known as unsecured loans.[48]

39 Ibid, Section 5(b).
40 Ibid, Section 5(c).
41 Ibid, Section 5(d).
42 Ibid, Section 5(dd).
43 Ibid, Section 5(e).
44 Ibid, Section 5(ee).
45 Ibid, Section 5(f).
46 Ibid, Section 5(ffa).
47 Ibid, Section 5(gg).
48 Ibid, Section 5(m).

### *3.4.1 Ordinance to Override Memorandum*

If the memorandum of a banking company, contracts executed, a resolution passed in the general meeting or by the directors of the company are repugnant to the Banking Companies Ordinance, 1962, they will not be legitimate.[49]

### *3.4.2 Use of the Word "Bank"*

No company can contain the word "bank" or any other name which indicates that it is a banking company if it is not carrying out the business of banking.[50]

### *3.4.3 Prohibition of Trade*

No banking company of Pakistan can be involved in any business of trading activities other than the one described in section 7 of the same ordinance.[51]

### *3.4.4 Restriction on Removal of Records and Documents*

All the banking companies which are being operated in Pakistan are bound to obtain prior permission from the SBP if they want to move any of their business records outside Pakistan which include ledgers, daybooks, cash books, account books and other documents they use for the purpose of their business.[52]

### *3.4.5 Requirement of Minimum Capital*

No banking company can carry out business in Pakistan unless it maintains the minimum capital requirement fixed by the SBP. A banking company that is not incorporated in Pakistan will have to maintain a minimum capital requirement by having deposits in the SBP via the transfer of foreign funds.[53]

### *3.4.6 Election of New Directors*

The State Bank of Pakistan is empowered to direct a banking company to call a meeting of all of its shareholders in a given time not less than two months to conduct fresh elections and elect new directors of the company. Directors can hold the office for a time their predecessor had or till the new election.

49 Ibid, Section 6(a)(b).
50 Ibid, Section 8(a)(b).
51 Ibid, Section 9.
52 Ibid, Section 12.
53 Ibid, Section 13.

Elections that are duly conducted under this section cannot be challenged in any court. Notwithstanding, SBP is authorised to appoint not more than one director in the banking company, even if it is repugnant to the memorandum of the company. Directors elected through the election or appointed by the SBP cannot hold their offices for more than six consecutive years.[54]

### 3.4.7 Cash Reserve

Every banking company incorporated in Pakistan which is not a scheduled bank is obligated to maintain, in the form of cash reserve, with itself or through a current account in the SBP or partly in cash and partly in such account, equivalent to at least 2 percent of its time liabilities and 5 percent of its demand liabilities in Pakistan.[55]

### 3.4.8 Restriction on Loans and Advances

No banking company is allowed to offer loans or advance against its securities. No loans or advances can be made on the guarantee of any of the director, family member of the director, any firm or private person in which the banking company or the director or family member of the director is a stakeholder. Moreover, it is also restricted for the banking company to lend loans to a director of the company or to a company or firm in which a director is a partner without getting approval from the majority of the directors excluding the concerned director.[56]

### 3.4.9 Power of the State Bank to Control Loans and Advance

The SBP is authorised to step in if it finds it expedient for the interest of the public to give a policy for loans and advances for the banking companies in general or a banking company in particular. All the banking companies or a particular banking company are bound to comply with that policy determined by the SBP in such context.[57]

### 3.4.10 Power of the State Bank to Collect and Furnish Credit Information

It is mandatory for all banking companies to furnish credit information to the SBP, which can, in its motion or at the request of any banking company, make

54 Ibid, Section 15.
55 Ibid, Section 22.
56 Ibid, Section 24.
57 Ibid, Section 25.

this information available on the payment of the fee SBP may fix from time to time.[58]

### *3.4.11 Preparation of Special Reports*

To ensure transparency and update the government regarding the financial condition of the country, the SBP is obliged to prepare special reports yearly, in which it provides all the details of the loans, banking securities of domestic and foreign banks and their advances to the federal government.[59]

### *3.4.12 Power of the State Bank not to Accept Deposits from the Banking Companies not Incorporated in Pakistan*

The SBP is empowered to declare in an official notification, which may be in the form of an official gazette, that it will not accept any deposits bearing interests from the date mentioned in the gazette from the banking companies incorporated outside Pakistan. However, such notification cannot be effected immediately or from a date less than six months from the date of the notification.[60]

### *3.4.13 Deposits*

The banking companies will receive deposits for the purpose that depositors will share in profit and loss. Domestic operations of the companies will remain interest-free until the federal government officially notifies the official gazette otherwise. The person or company who is depositing money based on sharing the profit and losses will also be bound to comply with the directions which SBP may give.[61]

### *3.4.14 Licensing of Banking Company*

To operate a banking company in Pakistan, all individuals or companies must obtain a license from the SBP. The license can be issued in some conditions. SBP is empowered to require certain assurance from the company or individual seeking the license that they are in a position to return the money of its current and future depositors on their demand. Assurance of not getting involved in a business that can harm the interest of its depositors can also be

58 Ibid, Section 25A.
59 Ibid, Section 25AA.
60 Ibid, Section 26(1)(2).
61 Ibid, Section 26A.

required. The SBP is authorised to cancel a license of a banking company if it will not comply with the rules and regulations to carry out this business. However, if it is not a matter of urgency for the interest of the depositors or the public at large, the SBP is bound to grant sufficient time to the concerned banking company so that it can comply with the rules and regulations. The banking company has the right to file an appeal, within 30 days, to the Central Board of State Bank (CBSB) against the cancellation of the license. Nonetheless, the decision of the CBSB will be administratively final. However, it can be challenged in a competent court of law.[62]

### 3.4.15 *Maintenance of Liquid Assets*

It is essential for every banking company operating in Pakistan to maintain liquid assets, which can be in the form of cash, gold or unencumbered, approved securities in Pakistan. The value of such liquidated assets should not be less than the total liabilities of the company in Pakistan at any time.[63]

### 3.4.16 *Responsibilities of the State Bank*

The SBP is obliged to have surveillance on all banking companies and ensure that all the banking companies which are operating in the financial system of Pakistan are abiding by the imposed rules and regulations for carrying out this business. It is the duty of the SBP to inform the federal government every quarter or even more frequently, if it is necessary, regarding the banking system, and the government can take timely actions to prevent a major loss.[64]

### 3.4.17 *Islamic Banking*

To establish an Islamic bank in Pakistan, it is obligated to strictly follow the injunctions of Islam described in the Holy Quran and Sunnah. The transactions of Islamic banking shall be interest-free. Conventional banks are also allowed to operate Islamic banking branches if they will comply with the rules and regulations set for Islamic banking as subsidiaries branches.[65] Apart from the difference in operation from conventional banks, Islamic banks are carrying out their business on an interest-free basis. All other obligations are the same for the banking companies and SBP also possesses the same powers and obligations for Islamic banking in Pakistan.

62 Ibid, Section 27(1–6).
63 Ibid, Section 29.
64 Ibid, Section 40A.
65 In sub-section (1) of section 23 of the Banking Companies Ordinance.

## 3.5 Financial Crisis and Basel Accord I, II and III

The financial crisis and severe losses in banking sectors across the global hauled the contentions towards the solution of the economic crisis. Empirical research to unfold the causes of financial unrest enlightened that the collapse of the banking sector had played a vital role to ignite recession. A financial crisis is not like a natural disaster that occurred surprisingly, but it always has reasons and cautions for befalling. In the modern economic system, the causes of the financial crisis can be domestic and international. The collapse of international banking and multinational companies can harm the economic system of a country that is growing otherwise. Policymakers around the globe are striving to make plausible regulations that can curtail the vulnerability of the economic systems.[66] Before explicating the salient features and contemporary significance of the Basel Accord, it is imperative to investigate the causes and consequences of the financial crisis.

### *3.5.1 Financial Crisis*

Surging demand for money creates a situation in which depositors start withdrawing their money from banks which causes a liquidity shortage. Usually, banks sell their illiquid assets to fulfil the demand for liquidity. However, the failure of the banks to handle the situation causes financial unrest, which can drag the entire economic system towards a financial crisis. Financial crises can be caused by several reasons, but mostly a panic among the investors or a major bank run becomes the main reason behind a crisis. After the Great Depression (1929), the financial crisis of 2007–2008 was the worst, which mainly occurred because of the collapse of the banking system.[67] However, it was argued by many economists that the Community Development Act, 1974, which ordained the banks to reduce their credit check requirements, played a vital role in creating a financial crisis.[68] A "financial crisis" is a generic term that is used for a situation of financial unrest. It can be further divided into six parts.

### *3.5.2 Currency Crisis*

Many countries use a fixed exchange rate, and in a situation where the currency valuation becomes unsustainable in the foreign exchange markets.

66 Dusan Baran, "Causes and Consequences of the Global Economic Crisis in the Present Period and Its Impact on the Slovak Republic" (22nd Australian Finance and Banking Conference) (August 25, 2009), Accessed: September 05, 2018.

67 S. Pelin Berkmen, Gaston Gelos, Robert K. Rennhack and James P. Walsh, "The Global Financial Crisis: Explaining Cross-Country Differences in the Output Impact" (January 05, 2010) IMF Working Paper No. 09/280, Accessed: September 05, 2018.

68 Ibid.

Sometimes, the investors start violating the official fixed rate, which puts immense pressure on the economic system and creates a panic among the investors. Consequently, the currency loses its value in the foreign markets, which affects the traders adversely. Deterioration in the values of the currency curtails foreign investment and increases the prices of everything in the country. A currency crisis makes the economic system vulnerable and curbs the capacity of the system to deter a recession. Turkey and Pakistan have faced the currency crisis in the recent past, which has had an adverse and long-lasting impact on the financial systems of both countries.[69]

### *3.5.3 External Debt Crisis*

The external debt crisis usually happens when a country is facing a current account deficit, which means a country is unable to make a balance in the flow of money. In other words, it is a situation in which the country's imports drastically increase, in contrast to its exports. It occurs when the country is unable to produce the capital to avert a current account deficit. The collapse of foreign reserves can also be a vital cause of the external debt crisis in this situation; the country immediately needs a bailout package to maintain the balance of payment. However, a bailout can only be a temporary solution to this crisis because the money will continuously be going out from the system; the bailout will be unhandy to maintain the sustainability of the system. This crisis can also happen due to the currency crisis because the devaluation of the currency will make it harder to maintain the balance of payment.[70]

### *3.5.4 Sovereign Debt Crisis*

A sovereign debt crisis is a situation where the government obtains loans from external means to clear its fiscal deficits and is unable to produce sufficient capital to return this debt and interest. This is a situation in which the government itself faces a financial crisis and is unable to cover its financial liabilities. Normally, the government, through the CB, lends liquidity to the financial institutions which are unable to fulfil the demand of liquidity by utilising all of their resources.[71]

69 Razvan Stefanescu and Dumitriu Ramona, "Impact of the Foreign Exchange Rates Fluctuations on Returns and Volatility of the Bucharest Stock Exchange" (Proceedings of the 5th International Conference on Economics and Administration No. 2) (2013), Page No. 197–209.

70 Rashid Zaman and Muhammad Arslan, "The Role of External Debt on the Economic Growth: Evidence from Pakistan Economy" (2014) *Journal of Economics and Sustainable Development*, Vol. 5, No. 24, Page No. 27.

71 Viral V. Acharya, Tim Eisert, Christian Eufinger and Christian W. Hirsch, "Real Effects of the Sovereign Debt Crisis in Europe: Evidence from Syndicated Loans" (Social Science Research Network, February 05, 2018), Accessed: September 07, 2018.

However, when the government is unable to pay back the loans and interests, it requires emergency financial lending by the IMF or any other external means. In such conditions, governments usually increase taxes, which causes inflation. Greece is a befitting example that obtained three bailouts in 2010 just to repay the loans and interests of the government. This is a worse situation for an economic system to sustain and be prosperous when the government requires more loans to clear earlier ones. A sovereign debt crisis can also be converted into a major financial crisis in the country.[72]

### *3.5.5 Banking Crisis*

The banking crisis occurs mainly due to the governance issues in general and loss of trust by the depositors in specific. The banking system can be regarded as the backbone of the economic system in this modern era. Banks are extensively involved in financial activities, and many financial institutions are also relying on it. Without having fortitude in the political and economic system, it is not possible to establish a strong baking system. Banks, across the globe, are playing a key role in the economic growth of the countries. Financial institutions lend liquidity from banks when they face a liquidity crisis, which helps them to get rid of the anxiety of liquidity issues.[73]

However, if the banking system of a country starts facing a crisis, it puts the sustainability of the entire economic system of the country at risk. In a banking crisis, investors desperately start taking their money out from the system, which urges the banks to sell their illiquid assets quickly to fulfil the demand for liquidity. Moreover, the quick sale of assets drops the value of the assets and makes the situation worse. The collapse of the banking system of Italy and Cyprus can be used as an example to appraise the effects of the banking crisis, which eventually led to a major financial crisis.[74]

### *3.5.6 Household Debt Crisis*

A household debt crisis can also be converted into a major financial crisis. In the UK and USA, the household debt crisis was surged and researched at a stage where it badly affects the financial system and plays its role along with

72 Filippo De Marco, "Bank Lending and the European Sovereign Debt Crisis" (July 22, 2017) *Journal of Financial and Quantitative Analysis*, Vol. 54, Accessed: September 07, 2018.

73 Boubacar Siddy Diallo, "The Role of the Banking Sector and Financial Markets on Economic Development" (February 2015) <https://core.ac.uk/download/pdf/77617774.pdf>, Accessed: September 08, 2018.

74 Mehmed Ganic, "The Impact of the Global Financial Crisis on the Banking Sector of Western Balkans: Cross-Country Analysis" (2012) *Journal of Economic and Social Studies*, Vol. 2, No. 2, Page No. 45.

other factors to cause the financial crisis of 2007–2008. It is a crisis in which people are unable to pay their mortgage, personal loans and credit card dues. The Basel Accord I and II allowed the banks to involve in risky mortgages and became a major cause of the financial crisis. All these different types of crises are interlinked because when the people will not pay their loans back or will not be able to pay the interests back to the banks, they will start facing a crisis. The banking crisis harms the entire economic system of the country; resultantly, the income of the government decreases, which can create a sovereign debt crisis or external debt crisis.[75]

### *3.5.7* ***Broad Financial Crisis***

This is a crisis that can be caused due to the combination of any of the previously mentioned crises or it can be a situation in which one crisis becomes the reason for another crisis. Several countries have faced these crises; for example, Mexico in 1994, Russia in 1996–1997, Argentine in 2001, and China in 2015 have faced financial crises, which were caused by more than one reason, and hence, can be termed as a broad financial crisis. To avoid such a financial crisis, significant changes have been made in the regulations relating to financial systems at the domestic and international levels.[76] Financial crises are now becoming common and frequent in the world, and these are happening all over the world; therefore, a particular country's legislation cannot be blamed for it. There are many reasons for the financial crises because the financial systems are becoming more equivocal and larger than they were before. However, they can be managed through proper regulatory frameworks.[77] Basel Accord III is aiming to curtail the panic of the financial crises, which will be explained in the next part of this chapter.

## 3.6 The Repercussion of the Financial Crisis

Financial crises always have effacing effects not only on economic systems but on society as well. In the modern economic system, where the financial systems have more financial institutions than before and the operating methods are also nebulous, the causes of a financial crisis occurring also surge. The main causes of a financial crisis were elucidated previously, which normally creates a situation where it becomes impossible for the financial system to

75 Tobias Adrian and Hyun Song Shin, "The Shadow Banking System: Implications for Financial Regulation" (2009) FRB of New York Staff Report No. 382.

76 Matthew Oxenford, "The Lasting Effects of the Financial Crisis Have Yet to Be Felt" (January 12, 2018) <https://georgetownsecuritystudiesreview.org/2019/11/19/everyone-loses-from-the-current-rise-in-protectionism/>, Accessed: September 10, 2018.

77 Ibid.

survive without the intervention of an external lender.[78] It is not possible to get rid of the effects of a financial crisis overnight because it always has a long-lasting impact on the system. The financial crisis does not occur accidentally; instead, it happens due to bad governance and failure of the regulatory frameworks. Although it is indefensible to argue that financial crises have no adverse effects on developing countries, it was realised after the recent financial crisis of 2007–2008 that it had more detrimental impacts on developing countries.[79]

The domestic market of a country seeks assistance from the government when they face financial issues. Normally, the CBs play the role of LOLR and lend liquidity to the financial institutions on the required stipulations. However, if the dread regarding the failure of the economic system disseminates among investors, it makes the system more vulnerable for the financial crisis to harm it because they start withdrawing their money. The sustainability of the financial system is directly proportionate to the trust of the debtors, and it is the responsibility of the CB to ensure that it has the capacity to lend frequently during panic and deter a financial crisis.[80] The failure of the CB to maintain the trust of the investors starts kicking out the investment from the system and minimises foreign investment and remittances. The immediate effect which a financial crisis causes is unemployment. Increasing unemployment puts a lot of pressure on the government and leaves adverse effects on society, and it takes several years to get out of the after-effects of the crisis.[81]

The prices of all commodities drastically increase in a financial crisis, and it leaves no room for the government to subsidise it. It damages low-income countries badly, in contrast to developing countries. The financial crisis coerces the government to seek assistance from external lenders to overcome the financial challenges; however, the aid or debt normally comes with tough conditions. IMF is playing the role of an international lender, but it is always a point of criticism by many economists across the globe that the IMF tries to influence the political and economic system of the states which seek assistance from it.[82] Governments take foreign loans to handle financial challenges; however, returning these loans and interests compel the government

78 Mehmed Ganic, "The Impact of the Global Financial Crisis on the Banking Sector of Western Balkans: Cross-Country Analysis" (2012) *Journal of Economic and Social Studies*, Vol. 2, No. 2, Page No. 21.

79 Justin Y. Lin and Will J. Martin, "The Financial Crisis and Its Impacts on Global Agriculture" (2016) World Bank Policy Research Working Paper No. 5431.

80 Viral V. Acharya and Matthew P. Richardson, "Causes of the Financial Crisis" (2009) *Critical Review*, Vol. 21, No. 2–3, Page No. 195–210.

81 Nicholas Oulton and Maria Sebastia-Barriel, "Long and Short-Term Effects of the Financial Crisis on Labour Productivity, Capital and Output" (2013) Bank of England Working Paper No. 470.

82 Myriam Senn, "The Impact of the Financial Crisis – Institutional Issues" (June 11–12, 2010) 6th Global Administrative Law Conference, Page No. 27.

to increase taxes, which has an adverse impact on the poor. Finally, the worse thing about a financial crisis is that it lasts for a long time. Notwithstanding, efficient financial policies and regulations which can handle the challenges of modern economic systems not only can help to curtail the effects of the financial crisis but will be helpful to deter further crisis.[83]

## 3.7 Background of the Basel Accord

Banks play a vigorous role in maintaining financial stability and immensely contribute to the GDP of financial systems at the domestic and international levels. In the modern economic era, banks have turned out to be an indispensable part of the financial system. However, loopholes in regulations allow the banking industry to become involved in risky financial activities, which can create a financial crisis.[84] The banks around the globe have played an important role in economic growth; however, due to an inappropriate legal system, the banking industry has caused financial crises. Thus, many countries have implemented mandatory deposit insurance policies to secure the deposit of the investors, but nothing has worked as a perpetual solution. After the collapse of several banks around the globe, the G10[85] group established the CB of Governors in 1975, which constituted a committee (the Basel Committee) to propose a solution for the banking system.[86]

The Basel Committee proposed a regulation to minimise risk, but this could not work because the method used by the Basel Committee to evaluate risk was obsolete. Therefore, the Basel Acord I was amended in November 1991 to tackle the challenges. Many lacunas existed in the Basel I regulations; hence, the Basel Committee introduced Basel II in June 1999. Basel II was esteemed to be a good regulation for preventing a financial crisis. However, major concerns regarding its capacity arose after the financial meltdown of 2007–2008. Thus, the Basel Committee introduced Basel III, which is yet to be implemented.[87]

Initially, only the G10 formed the Basel Committee, but later, they enhanced their membership, and now, more than 28 countries are members of

83 Wilson N. Sy, "Implications of the Global Financial Crisis" (2015) *Journal of the Economics and Business Educators NSW*, No. 2, Page No. 26–34.

84 C. W. Calomiris and G. Gorton, "The Origins of Banking Panics: Models, Facts, and Bank Regulation", *Financial Markets and Financial Crises* (University of Chicago Press, 1991), Page No. 109–74.

85 Belgium, Canada, France, Germany, Italy, Japan, Luxemburg, Netherlands, Spain, Sweden, Switzerland, the UK, and the US.

86 C. Goodhart, *The Basel Committee on Banking Supervision: A History of the Early Years, 1974–1997* (Cambridge University Press, 2011).

87 A. Toor, "International Financial Regulation and the Basel Accord: How the Impact of a Soft Law Whisper Results in Compliance Throughout the Global" (May 23, 2017) SSRN, Accessed: October 29, 2018.

the Committee.[88] Although there are no direct repercussions for the member countries if they refuse to implement the regulation proposed by the Committee, it has still been adopted by many countries. The Basel Accord is regarded as a soft international law because, unlike international regulations, there are no substantial consequences for not implementing it. However, there is an indirect repercussion for the country that does not implement the suggestions of the Committee because foreign investors and banks will be reluctant to invest. However, the implementation of Basel's suggestions can reassure investors that the financial system is sound and there will be no risk of a financial meltdown.[89]

### *3.7.1 Basel Accord I*

The banking sector took a prospective start and, due to its profitability, it grabbed the attention of both public and private investors. Several banks in the United States, Bankhaus in Germany and Long Island's Franklin National Bank collapsed in the 1970s. Although the Federal Reserve tried to frame a regulation that could prevent the failure of the banking system, it could not stop the banks from avoiding this regulation.[90]

- The Basel Accord is considered a major milestone in the history of the banking system because it proposed a minimum capital standard for banks around the globe. Member countries of the Basel Committee agreed to set a minimum capital requirement of 8 percent of risk-weighted assets for all internationally active banks in their jurisdictions. Bank capital was also defined in Basel I. The minimum capital requirement was proposed because the banks already held a low level of capital, which declined further due to the increase of off-balance-sheet activities. Another reason behind setting the minimum capital requirement was the desire of the banks of some jurisdictions to obtain a short-term competitive advantage in financial markets. They were maintaining a very low level of capital to get this advantage, and this turned out to be a serious problem for the financial systems.[91]

88 Bank for International Settlement, "Basel Committee on Banking Supervision: A Brief History of the Basel Committee" (October 2014) Bank for International Settlement, Accessed: November 01, 2017.

89 A. Toor, "International Financial Regulation and the Basel Accord: How the Impact of a Soft Law Whisper Results in Compliance Throughout the Global" (May 23, 2017) SSRN, Accessed: October 29, 2018.

90 P. Jackson, "Bank Capital Standards: The New Basel Accord" (Spring 2001) Bank of England Quarterly Bulletin, Accessed: September 17, 2018.

91 A. Toor, "International Financial Regulation and the Basel Accord: How the Impact of a Soft Law Whisper Results in Compliance Throughout the Global" (May 23, 2017) SSRN, Accessed: October 29, 2018.

- The minimum capital requirement set by Basel Acord asked the banks to generate more capital to fulfil the requirement. However, during the 1990s, banks developed various techniques to undermine the riskiness of different parts of their portfolio and introduced a new category of economic capital. Consequently, discrepancies arose between the minimum required capital and economic capital, which allowed the banks to avoid regulatory requirements.[92]
- To fulfil the requirement of minimum capital, the banks started turning to securitisation schemes. Thus, until 1998, the outstanding securitisation was more than $200 billion on behalf of the ten largest banks of the United States. All these strategies resulted in the failure of Basel I to maintain the capital requirement internationally. Additionally, there were no proper standards to recognise the level of risk attached to the financial activities of the banks. Basel Accord I's scope was also limited for evaluating the reduction of risk in the presence of worthy collaterals, which hindered the banks from taking advantage of it.[93]
- All these issues of capital requirement and the inability of the Accord to recognise the reduction of risk through collaterals put pressure on the Basel Committee. Thus, the Committee amended the regulation in 1996 and allowed the banks to use value at risk models for the recognition of the reduction of risk.[94]
- Finally, although there were major loopholes in the regulatory framework of Basel Accord I, it was still adopted by member nations of the Basel Committee and some other countries as well.

### *3.7.2 Basel Accord II*

The Basel Committee tried to address the lacunas of Basel I, and so, they made a major amendment to it. They tried to comprehend new techniques that had been developed by banking officials. However, the changes made by the amendment were not sufficient enough to address the issues. The Basel Committee was pressurised to allow the banks to use credit risk models for fulfilling the capital requirement, but the Committee was unsure regarding the accuracy of these models. Research carried out by the Bank of England indicated that the model of credit risk was at a very early stage of development. Hence, the Committee had to propose a new regulation to address the

92 P. Jackson, "Bank Capital Standards: The New Basel Accord" (Spring 2001) Bank of England Quarterly Bulletin, Accessed: September 17, 2018.

93 J. Bhowmik and S. Tewari, "Basel Accord and the Failure of Global Trust Bank: A Case Study" (2010) *The IUP Journal of Bank Management*, Vol. 9, No. 3, Page No. 37–62.

94 P. Jackson, "Bank Capital Standards: The New Basel Accord" (Spring 2001) Bank of England Quarterly Bulletin, Accessed: September 17, 2018.

issue and comply with contemporary issues of the capital requirement and assessment of the riskiness attached to the financial activities of the banking industry.[95]

- Although Basel II came a few months before the financial crisis of 2007–2008 hit the financial markets, it was still blamed by many economists for not averting the crisis. Basel II was proposed to address the loopholes of Basel I and framed an advanced financial regulation. The failure of the method of calculating capital and recognising the risk reduction in the presence of collaterals urged the Basel Committee to repeal Basel I and propose a new Accord. Only one method had been used to calculate capital by Basel I; however, three methods were proposed in Basel II.

a) **Standardised Approach**
The Standardised Approach was not a new method used in Basel II, as it was also used in Basel I. However, it was altered according to the requirements of the modern banking system. According to this method, a fixed percentage of risk was used after assessing the financial markets. For example, a 35-percent risk was fixed for the residential loans in Basel II. Similarly, according to the nature of the business, the risk was predetermined and fixed for all types of financial activities.[96]

b) **Foundation of the International Rating Approach**
This was a new approach proposed in Basel II, which empowered the lender to determine the risk attached to financial activities and required a respective amount of minimum capital. The acumen behind offering this approach for the capital requirement was that the lenders had a maximum stake in the stability of the system, and so, would not allow the banks to become involved in risky activities without holding sufficient capital. Nonetheless, this approach allowed the banks to play with their lenders and avoid the minimum capital requirement by undermining the risk because, normally, the depositors had no parameters to determine it. Basel II was criticised by many economists after the financial crisis due to this approach.[97]

c) **Advanced Internal Rating Approach**
This method was also initially proposed in Basel II, by which the lenders had to determine the probability of default, loss given default and exposure at default. This method was used because it could swiftly determine the

95 K. Dowd, M. O. Hutchinson and S. G. Ashby, "Capital Inadequacies: The Dismal Failure of the Basel Regime of Bank Capital Regulation" (July 2011) Cato Institute Policy Analysis No. 681, Accessed: July 07, 2018.

96 P. Jackson, "Bank Capital Standards: The New Basel Accord" (Spring 2001) Bank of England Quarterly Bulletin, Accessed: September 17, 2018.

97 Bank for International Settlement, "Basel Committee on Banking Supervision: A Brief History of the Basel Committee" (October 2014) Bank for International Settlement, Accessed: November 01, 2017.

risk attached and help the lender recognise the requirements of the capital. Banks used their own loss probabilities models in this approach.[98]

- Basel Accord I could not address operational risk, but Basel II did address this issue. Operational risk is a kind of risk attached to the operation of the banks while undertaking a financial activity. Basel II was not aimed merely at implementing new capital rules. Rather, it was mandated to increase the quality of risk management and supervision. Basel II introduced three pillars for its regulatory framework. Pillar I elucidated the minimum capital requirement. Pillar II was a supervisory review allowing the supervisors to cross-check if the banks' assessment regarding risk was reasonable. Mere reliance on the minimum capital requirement defined under Pillar I was not sufficient, so the banks and the supervisors must understand the risk profile and capitalise it accordingly. Pillar III was a market discipline that enhanced transparency in the banks' financial reports.[99]

### *3.7.3 Basel Accord III*

Basel II addressed the lacunas of Basel I and tried to comprehend the needs of the modern banking system. New techniques were also defined in Basel II to recognise the capital requirement for banks. The financial crisis of 2007–2008 is regarded as the worst crisis in the history of financial crises after the Great Depression. This financial crisis harmed the entire world badly, but it changed the mindset of the policymakers and urged them to consider the proposals of the Basel Accord and LOLR as an essential part of the financial systems to strengthen them against the crisis. The collapse of Lehman Brothers (September 2008) was seriously contentious and highlighted the loopholes of Basel II. Additionally, the detrimental effects of the crisis led the Basel Committee towards a new regulation: Basel III.[100]

- The capital requirement for commercial banks was revised in September 2010, which later turned out to be part of Basel III. The causes of the financial crisis were deliberated in depth; all possible loopholes were identified and addressed by the Basel Committee in Basel III. It was recognised by the Committee that Basel I and Basel II were not implemented properly in many states, which had contributed to the crisis. Thus,

98 Basel Committee on Banking Supervision, *Consultative Documents: The International Rating-Based Approach* (Basel Committee on Banking Supervision, May 31, 2001), Accessed: October 30, 2018.

99 S. Venkataraman, "Integrated Risk Management Framework and Basel II" (February 24, 2006) SSRN, Accessed: May 11, 2018.

100 E. Lee, "Basel III and Its New Capital Requirements, as Distinguished from Basel II" (2014) *The Banking Law Journal University of Hong Kong Faculty of Law*, Vol. 131, No. 1, Page No. 27–69.

27 states announced that they would start implementing Basel III on 1 January 2013.[101]

- The three main pillars of Basel II were re-formed in Basel III. For common equity, the minimum capital requirement was 2 percent in Basel II, which increased to 3.5 percent in Basel III. For Tier I, the minimum capital requirement was 4 percent, which increased to 4.5 percent. The term "bank" was explicitly elucidated in Basel III. For all risk-weighted assets, the minimum capital requirement was declared to be 8 percent. "Capital buffer" was a new term to use in the banking system as defined in Basel III, which can be calculated as:

  i) Available Capital – Risk Capital = Capital Buffer[102]

- After the proposals of Basel III, many economists voiced their concerns that it will not be able to prevent further financial crisis and argues that it would be a tough task for the banks to meet the minimum capital requirement set by Basel III. The banking systems of small economies would not be able to meet the capital standards, and so, they would not be able to implement them. Basel III tries to enhance the level of communication among banks and to improve transparency to help evaluate riskiness accurately.[103]

## 3.8 Implementation Challenges of the Basel Accord in Pakistan

Although 27 states were committed to fully implement Basel III from 1 January 2013, according to the report of the Basel Committee published in April 2013, only 11 states could implement it. Not only do countries with small economies struggle to implement it, but countries like Canada are also struggling. They passed rules to implement the framework of the Basel Accord in December 2012, but they were not able to implement them until January 2014.[104] Moreover, developed countries like the United States adopted a different method to implement the framework of the Basel Accord.

101 M. R. Saidenberg and T. Schuermann, "The New Basel Accord and Questions for Research" (June 2013) Wharton Financial Institutions Center Working Paper No. 03–14, Accessed: October 31, 2018.

102 E. Lee, "Basel III and Its New Capital Requirements, as Distinguished from Basel II" (2014) *The Banking Law Journal University of Hong Kong Faculty of Law*, Vol. 131, No. 1, Page No. 27–69.

103 J. K. M. Mawutor, "Analysis of Basel III and Risk Management in Banking" (2014) *European Journal of Business Management*, Vol. 6, Page No. 6.

104 A. Gurrea-Martinez and N. Remolina, "The Dark Side of the Implementation of Basel Capital Requirement: Theory, Evidence and Policy" (October 18, 2017) SSRN, Accessed: April 13, 2018.

The Dodd-Frank Wall Street reforms and the Consumer Protection Act were used to implement it at the domestic level. The Capital Requirement Regulation (CRR) and the Capital Requirement Directive (27 June 2013) were mandated to implement Basel III in Europe. The CRR is now part of the domestic law in all member states. Basel III is not a regulation for the banking system alone; it also covers all the financial institutions. However, some states like Switzerland have set an even higher capital requirement for their banking systems to minimise the dread of insolvency.[105]

There is a split on the matter of capital standards in the EU because the United Kingdom and Sweden are of the view that the capital standards must be at the discretion of the State instead of having the same standard. However, Germany and France emphasise having the same capital standard in the EU States.[106] Pakistan is a country facing several economic and political challenges. It is listed as a developing economy and among countries having a small economy. For a country like Pakistan, it is not an easy task to implement the capital requirement regulations of Basel III immediately. It can take several years to fully implement Basel III. Pakistan, unlike many other developing countries, took serious initiatives to implement it. The SBP issued a circular (BPRD Circular No. 06, 2013), which was passed by the Parliament in 2013, mandating the implementation of the framework of Basel III in Pakistan.[107] Initially, this circular only addressed eligible capital, capital ratio and leverage ratio and explicitly stated that other parts of the framework of Basel III would be addressed separately. This circular, however, sends a resounding message to the financial institutions of Pakistan regarding its intentions to implement the framework of Basel III. The SBP set a deadline of 31 December 2019 to fully implement Basel III in all its banks and financial institutions.[108]

## 3.9 LOLR in the Perspective of Pakistan

The LOLR is also an imperative part of modern financial systems like the Basel Accord. The inception of the banking system has played an important role in the growth of financial systems at the domestic and international levels. However, avarice lured the business fraternity towards risky business activities, and the absence of efficient regulations caused the financial crisis. The failure of the domestic banking regulations and the detrimental effects of

105 M. Ojo, "Progress on Adoption of Basel III Standards: Monetary Policy, Leverage Ratio and Risk Based Capital Adequacy Measures" (March 08, 2018) SSRN, Accessed: April 15, 2018.

106 A. Gurrea-Martinez and N. Remolina, "The Dark Side of the Implementation of Basel Capital Requirement: Theory, Evidence and Policy" (October 18, 2017) SSRN, Accessed: April 13, 2018.

107 S. A. A. Shah, "Why Pakistani Banks Failed to Adopt Advance Approaches of Basel Accord According to Road Map of State Bank of Pakistan" (August 28, 2012) SSRN, Accessed: April 21, 2018.

108 O. Masood, "Risk Management and Basel-Accord-Implementation in Pakistan" (2017) *Journal of Financial Regulation and Compliance*, Vol. 20, No. 3, Page No. 111.

financial crises compelled policymakers to come out of their trance that the freedom of business for the banking sector was enhancing the growth of the economic system. It is, indeed, an undeniable fact that banks have contributed a great deal to financial growth.

Nonetheless, the damage which occurred due to the loopholes in the legislation relating to the banking system is also alarming. After the failure of many banks around the globe, the policymakers recognised the lacunas and realised the need for an international banking regulation, which eventually led them to the Basel Accord. The significance of the Basel Accord has been extensively described above. The Basel Accord is not simply an international banking regulation for the member states of the Basel Committee; rather, it is disseminated across the globe.[109]

At an earlier stage of the banking and financial evolution, the role of LOLR was not well accepted by the policymakers. It was regarded as a rescue package for larceners and criticised by economists as nothing but a waste of taxpayers' money. As the role of CBs evolved and financial crises of different eras badly damaged the world economy, the debate surged among policymakers regarding the need for a LOLR for the system. Initially, the understanding of the LOLR was nothing more than a rescue package in the form of liquidity or through buying the illiquid assets of the financial institutions which were facing the problem of insolvency. Until the financial crisis of 2007–2008, this role could not grab the attention of policymakers as an integral part of the financial system.[110]

Now, after a long process of deliberating on the causes of financial crises, it has been realised that the trust of the depositors is the key factor in deterring a crisis. However, if dread regarding the failure of the financial spreads among investors, they will immediately start demanding their money from the financial system. A surge in the demand for liquidity adversely affects the system and pushes financial institutions either to sell their illiquid assets swiftly or to seek the intervention of the CB in the form of LOLR. The presence of a LOLR assures the investors that the financial institution will not collapse, which helps the financial institutions keep the trust of their depositors.[111]

## 3.10 Legitimacy of LOLR in Pakistan

Pakistan has established its CB, known as State Bank of Pakistan, in 1948, which holds the power to emit new notes and plays the role of LOLR for its financial system. The banking industry took a slow start in Pakistan, and

109 M. D. Bordo, "Rules for a Lender of Last Resort: An Historical Perspective" (2014) *Journal of Economic Dynamics and Control*, Vol. 49, Accessed: February 02, 2019.

110 F. Capie, "Can There Be an International Lender of Last Resort?" (2002) *International Finance*, Vol. 1, No. 2, Page No. 15.

111 M. Berlemann, K. Hristov and N. Nenovsky, "Lending of Last Resort, Moral Hazard and Twin Crises Lessons from the Bulgarian Financial Crisis 1996/1997" (2002) <https://ideas.repec.org/p/hal/journl/halshs-00260241.html>, Accessed: February 10, 2018.

different banking policies were deployed to make a modern banking system. Pakistan is among those countries which have two entirely different banking systems: the conventional and Islamic banking systems. Pakistan is a developing country where the laws relating to the banking sector are still in the process of evolution. Tentative financial conditions and major financial crises have urged the policymakers of Pakistan to comply with the international banking regulation of the Basel Accord and address the lacunas of its domestic legislation.

The SBP is empowered through the State Bank of Pakistan Act, 1956 to play the role of LOLR for the financial institutions which are facing the problems of liquidity. The SBP has played this role for several financial institutions and provided liquidity. However, the absence of strong regulation and a frequency in playing the role of LOLR made it difficult for the SBP to survive. Thus, Pakistan sought the intervention of the international LOLR (ILOLR) and obtained a rescue package from IMF, which plays the role of ILOLR.[112] There is only one section regarding the role of LOLR in the SBPA, 1956 which empowers the SBP to play this role. However, a proper framework to regulate the operations of LOLR is still absent.

- If a scheduled bank starts facing a liquidity shortage and seeks assistance from the State Bank of Pakistan, the SBP may lend liquidity after recognising that the bank is solvent and has the capacity to provide adequate collateral.[113]

The laws which authorised the SBP to play the role of LOLR have not left it merely on the discretionary powers of SBP either to lend liquidity support or not. Walter Bagehot is among the few of them who played an imperative role in introducing the legal framework of LOLR. He had proposed the basic rules for the CBs, which should be followed while lending liquidity to the financial institutions. The CBs should only lend liquidity to the illiquid, however, solvent institutions. The liquidity support should only be limited to those financial institutions which can provide worthy collaterals. Finally, the support of liquidity should be encouraged, and that is why a high-interest rate should be charged as a penalty.[114]

Appraisal of the law which is regulating the role of LOLR in Pakistan gives the impression that the rules of Walter Bagehot are followed. These were proposed in an era when the presence of LOLR was objected to by many economists that it was a package for those who were not performing their

112 Sara Cheema, "The IMF: Pakistan's History and Future with the LOLR", *Eurasia Review* (June 19, 2017), Accessed: November 04, 2018.

113 Section 17G of the State Bank of Pakistan Act, 1956.

114 Robert E. Keleher and Thomas M. Humphery, "The Lender of Last Resort: A Historical Perspective" (1984) *Cato Journal*, Vol. 4, No. 1, Page No. 275.

duties. However, in modern times, the financial needs are different and the role of LOLR also emerges a lot. These rules are still playing an important role; however, on many occasions, even the Bank of England operated as LOLR and superseded these rules.[115]

### *3.10.1 The LOLR for Islamic Banks*

The operations of LOLR are based on high-interest rates as a penalty around the globe; no liquidity support comes free because it is against the basic rule of having a LOLR. Even the liquidity which the SBP has obtained at different times from the International Monetary Fund (IMF) is based on high-interest rates. The conventional banks work on the interest-based system in Pakistan. However, the Islamic banking system claims to operate as an interest-free industry. The conditions under which the role of LOLR could be played for the Islamic banks are still under deliberation. In Pakistan, the understanding of LOLR still revolves around the concept that any financial institution which has liquidity in surplus can play the role of LOLR by lending liquidity to financial institutions that are experiencing problems of liquidity. Thus, the SBP has allowed conventional banks to open Sharia-compliant windows to act as LOLR for Islamic banks. *Sukuk* (Islamic bonds) have also been introduced to address this issue.[116]

Islamic banks are growing exceptionally well in Pakistan, but still, a deep evaluation of the history of financial crises divulges that LOLR is an integral part of the banking industry. The absence of LOLR can add to a trivial financial panic and convert it into a serious financial crisis. Therefore, it is still a milestone, not only to regulate but also to appoint a LOLR for Islamic banking that is compliant with Sharia law.[117] The Islamic banks operate as interest-free sectors, and they do not offer any fixed interest to their depositors and do not charge any interest from debtors. The SBP offers liquidity support based on interest-free grounds, which is charged as a penalty to discourage the financial institutions from obtaining it again and again. However, if the Islamic banks are offered liquidity support with no interest or penalty charged, it will encourage them to seek financial support frequently. The history of financial crises enunciates that a continuous engagement of the CB in lending liquidity as a LOLR causes a financial crisis. Hence, a system that can discourage

115 Mateen Altaf, "Role of State Bank of Pakistan in Economic Development of the Country" *Economy & Finance* (2016), Accessed: November 04, 2018.

116 S. Zaheer and M. Farooq, "Liquidity Crisis: Are Islamic Banking Institutions More Resilient?" Paper presented at the Joint RES-SPR Conference on Macroeconomic Challenges Facing Low-Income Countries Hosted by the International Monetary Fund (January 30–31, 2014), Accessed: November 04, 2018.

117 M. Umer, "Lender of Last Resort for Islamic Banks Under Review", *Dawn News* (April 01, 2015), Accessed: November 04, 2018.

Islamic banks from seeking liquidity support and comply with Sharia law remains undiscovered.[118]

## 3.11 Summary

The banking regime of Pakistan is explained in this chapter, and all the laws which regulate the banking industry are also described. The role of the banking sector in any financial system is appraised and argued on different policies that are used to establish a sound financial system in Pakistan. The effects of a financial crisis are enlightened. The Banking and Companies Ordinance, 1962 (LVII of 1962) is also discussed in detail, which is used to regulate the banking sector in Pakistan. Basel Accord is an international regulation for the banking system. The reasons for establishing a Basel Committee and loopholes in the Basel I and II are also illustrated in it. The implementation challenges of Basel III are examined and the steps which Pakistan took so far to implement Basel III are also evaluated. Finally, the role of LOLR is explicated in the context of Pakistan, and the laws which legitimise its functions are also appraised. The diversity of the banking system is also described, and the challenges which Pakistan is facing to establish a system of LOLR for the Islamic banks are also observed.

118 M. El Hamiani Khatat, "Monetary Policy in the Presence of Islamic Banking" (March 2016) IMF Working Paper 16/72, Accessed: November 04, 2018.

# 4 Case Study of Pakistan

The core purpose of this chapter in this book is to identify the problem in the regulatory system of Pakistan in the context of LOLR. The chapter also answers the research question of this research. It provides a detailed discussion on the operation of LOLR by the SBP to identify the problem. It argues that the power of acting as LOLR is allocated to the SBP after the financial crisis of 2007–2008. The SBP is empowered to act as LOLR through an amendment in the State Bank of Pakistan Act 1956 in 2015. The section is examined in this chapter. Furthermore, a case study of the KASB bank is examined to identify the problem. The establishment of the KASB is discussed besides the functioning of the bank until the merger took place. All of the legal formalities which were required to be fulfilled in the amalgamation of the KASB into the BankIslami are appraised. The chapter concludes by arguing that, although there are loopholes in the regulation, the main problem lies in the transparency issues while conducting the LOLR operations.

## 4.1 Case Study of the KASB Bank

To evaluate the role of the State Bank of Pakistan as a LOLR, a famous case of KASB Bank from recent times is befitting to appraise. KASB Bank was established in 1994 by Khadim Ali Shah Bukhari.[1] The main head office of the bank was in Karachi which is the largest city in Pakistan. The bank was established under the Banking and Companies Ordinance of 1962.[2] The legal formalities of establishing a banking company under this law are discussed in detail in Chapter 4 of this study. KASB group of companies owns the KASB Bank, which is regarded as one of the oldest capital markets in Pakistan. KASB group of companies was established in 1952 by Mr Khadim Ali Shah Bukhari. The bank was established to provide financial support to

1 Khadim Ali Shah Bukhari (Pvt) Ltd, <https://kasb.com/about/>, Accessed: March 21, 2020.

2 Shahbaz Rana, "Legal Formalities of Defunct KASB Bank Remain Unfulfilled", *The Express Tribune* (Pakistan, September 08, 2019).

DOI: 10.4324/9781003478768-4

the business fraternity of the country. KASB group of companies has a major contribution in real estate (KASB Tower), education (KASB Institute of Technology), agriculture and media industry.[3]

The CB of Pakistan, known as SBP, requires the banks working within the country to meet minimum capital requirements. Although Basel Accord III is not implemented yet in Pakistan, still, the banks which are operating in the country are under an obligation to maintain capital, which is required. Requirements of the capital and principles of Basel Accord III are briefly discussed in Chapter 4 of this study. To identify the problem in the LOLR operations, the merger of KASB is used as a case study. During the financial crisis of 2007–2008, the KASB Bank started facing liquidity problems.[4] In compliance with the rules of Basel to maintain stability in the banking sector, the SBP warned the bank to meet the regulatory capital requirement. The owner of the bank owns many other companies and tried to utilise their capital to meet the minimum capital requirement.[5]

Furthermore, the SBP placed the bank under a moratorium by using its regulatory powers. Rather than imparting liquidity to KASB Bank by following the rules of demanding collaterals and evaluating the solvency of the bank, the SBP allowed another bank to take over this bank.[6] This approach was not only unprecedented but also raised several questions. The SBP was accused of lack of transparency while using the regulatory powers. The report of the Auditor General of Pakistan on the merger of the bank also objected to the role of the CB.[7] The SBP allowed BankIslami to take over the KASB Bank because it failed to meet the regulatory capital requirement. Moreover, no liquidity was provided to the KASB Bank by imposing any of the conditions which could help the bank to get over the liquidity crisis. The SBP lent Rs. 5 billion (PKR) at (0.01 percent) to BankIslami, which resulted in litigation and embezzlement inquiries.[8] The Banking and Companies Ordinance 1962, which empowers the SBP to act as a regulator for the banking of Pakistan, also binds the government to present the report before the parliament and make it a public document.

"Copies of the scheme or any order made under sub-section (11) shall be laid on the table of the Legislature, as soon as may be, after the scheme has

3 Khadim Ali Shah Bukhari (Pvt) Ltd, <https://kasb.com/about/>, Accessed: March 21, 2020.

4 Muntazar Bashir Ahmed, "KASB Bank Limited: Capital Shortage", *Sage Journals* (Pakistan, March 05, 2018).

5 Khurram Hussain, "Analysis: The Little Bank That Couldn't", *Dawn Newspaper* (Pakistan, May 02, 2015).

6 Mian Abrar, "KASB Bank Merger – a Tale of Misplaced Priorities", *Pakistan Today* (May 09, 2015).

7 Muhammad Farooq, "AGP Says BankIslami-KASB Bank Merger Resulted in Rs. 3.5 Billion Loss to National Exchequer", *Pakistan Today* (April 01, 2018).

8 Shahbaz Rana, "Legal Formalities of Defunct KASB Bank Remain Unfulfilled", *The Express Tribune* (Pakistan, September 08, 2019).

been sanctioned by the Federal Government, or as the case may be, the order has been made".[9]

However, this report is not published nor presented before the parliament, which raised serious questions on the transparency of the role of LOLR of the SBP.[10] Moreover, the SBP lifted a moratorium from KASB immediately after its merger into BankIslami without giving appropriate reasons for it.[11]

The SBP Act, 1956 empowers the CB of the country to officially play the role of LOLR for the financial institutions at the domestic level which are experiencing financial troubles.[12]Although the Act stated the principles for carrying out the operations of LOLR, there was a lack of transparency in most of its LOLR operations due to heavy political influence on the management of the CB. Thus, not only this role of the SBP is controversial but it is also adversely affecting the financial system of the country. It is a fundamental principle of carrying out the LOLR operations that liquidity support should not be offered without following the basic principles. The lack of a proper regulatory framework allows the politician to influence the regulatory powers of the SBP, which resulted in severe moral hazard problems. Therefore, rather than strengthening the financial system through the assurance of liquidity support, the presence of LOLR is making the financial system more fragile.[13]

The State Bank of Pakistan lent liquidity to several commercial banks and State institutions which were unable to fulfil their financial liabilities.[14] Due to the unsatisfactory performance of the banking sector, Pakistan has implemented the policy of the nationalisation of financial institutions, including all commercial banks. The policy of nationalisation is discussed in detail in Chapter 5 of this book. In the early 1990s, many financial institutions, including Muslim Commercial Bank and Allied Bank, were privatised due to their bad performances. Most of the employees working in these banks were employed on a political basis. More than necessary employees were causing big losses to these banks.[15] Rather than the SBP, it was the Federal Government of Pakistan that decided to nationalise or privatise these financial institutions. The SBP has also acted as LOLR for the Government of Pakistan on

9 The Banking and Companies Ordinance 1962, Section 47(12)

10 Shahbaz Rana, "Legal Formalities of Defunct KASB Bank Remain Unfulfilled", *The Express Tribune* (Pakistan, September 08, 2019).

11 Mian Abrar, "KASB Bank Merger – a Tale of Misplaced Priorities", *Pakistan Today* (May 09, 2015).

12 The State Bank of Pakistan Act 1956, Section 17G.

13 Shahbaz Rana, "Legal Formalities of Defunct KASB Bank Remain Unfulfilled", *The Express Tribune* (Pakistan, September 08, 2019).

14 Arshad Ali, "The Impact of Financial Crisis on Pakistani Economy" (Winter 2008 & Spring 2009) *Strategic Studies*, Vol. 28, Page No. 106–17.

15 Prof Muhammad Ishaque Bajoi and Prof Dr Ambreen Zaib Khaskelly, "Privatization of Banking Sector in Pakistan- A Case Study of MCB Bank Limited" (2017) *International Journal of Management and Information Technology*, Vol. 12, No. 1, Page No. 3159–66, ISSN: 2278-5612.

several occasions.[16] There is no record available in the public domain for the rescue operations of the SBP because it was acting on the directions of the government. The SBP is empowered to regulate the banks working within the country and implement financial policy. However, as far as the role of LOLR is concerned, it is explicitly attributed to the SBP through an amendment in the State Bank of Pakistan Act, 1956 in 2015.[17] Therefore, the liquidity support to the financial institutions or the policy of nationalisation or privatisation of the banks is considered as national policy rather than the LOLR operations of the SBP. After the amendment in the State Bank of Pakistan Act 1956, there is a case of KASB, which has already been discussed previously. The doctrine of LOLR is yet to be properly evolved in the system of Pakistan.

There are some serious questions pertaining to the merger of the KASB Bank into BankIslami. The minimum capital requirement for the banks in Pakistan was increased by the SBP from 1 billion to 10 billion after the financial crisis of 2007–2008.[18] For this purpose, the KASB bank was pressurised by the SBP to meet the minimum capital requirement (MCR). The SBP holds the powers to act as LOLR or it can also exercise the powers to sell the bank. Notwithstanding, it is also imperative to consider that the KASB bank was working efficiently, despite its inability to fulfil the obligation of capital requirements.[19] There was no panic for the bank run nor were there any complaints regarding the dishonouring of the cheques in the bank. Furthermore, in 2014 the KASB bank was maintaining liquidity of 16 billion, which was the highest among its peer group. Nonetheless, the SBP opted to put a moratorium on it.[20] Although it is the duty of the CB as a regulator to ensure that all banks are complying with the requirement of MCR, it must not be partial in its operations.

Any bank which is working in a State and incorporates according to the laws of the land has some rights besides several obligations. The KASB Bank also possessed the right to seek liquidity support from the SBP by fulfilling the conditions. The LOLR powers were allocated to the SBP through an amendment in the State Bank of Pakistan Act 1956 in 2015. The merger of KASB also took place in the same year. The SBP, rather than using its LOLR powers, used other regulatory powers, in this case, which are unjust, ostensibly. The SBP does not hold any powers to restrict the right of any bank to seek liquidity from other sources, domestic or international. The KASB Bank managed to get liquidity

16 <http://www.sbp.org.pk/FS/4.4.asp>, Accessed: April 10, 2020.

17 State Bank of Pakistan (Amendment) Act, 2015.

18 Shahbaz Rana, "Legal Formalities of Defunct KASB Bank Remain Unfulfilled", *The Express Tribune* (Pakistan, September 08, 2019).

19 Asim Yasir, "Selling of KASB Bank to BI in Just RS 1000 Echoes in PAC Meeting", *International The News* (Pakistan, April 27, 2018).

20 Shahbaz Rana, "Legal Formalities of Defunct KASB Bank Remain Unfulfilled", *The Express Tribune* (Pakistan, September 08, 2019).

support of $100 million from a leading Chinese company to meet the MCR.[21] One of the largest leading commercial banks of the country, Muslim Commercial Bank, also showed its interest in buying the KASB Bank or injecting liquidity. However, both of the options were rejected by the SBP.[22] Additionally, had the Chinese company been allowed to buy the KASB Bank, a substantial amount of foreign currency would have been injected into the financial system of Pakistan. However, the SBP rejected the offer of the Chinese company named Cybernaut and stated that the functioning of the company is dubious.[23]

The KASB Bank filed a petition in the Islamabad High Court to restrain the SBP from selling the bank, which was accepted. In the petition, the KASB Bank promised to get liquidity and meet the MCR. On 20 April 2015, the bank managed to get an offer of $100 million from Cybernaut, a Chinese company that had an investment fund of $10 billion in China. A formal letter was submitted into the SBP, stating that the Chinese company will inject $100 million. The letter stated that $20 million will be injected before 13 May, a further $30 million will be injected in August and the remaining $50 million will be injected by the end of the year.[24] Subsequently, Khadim Ali Shah Bukhari, the owner of the bank, would become a minority shareholder, and the new name of the bank was proposed as Pak-China Bank.[25] On 21 April, after the submission of the offer to the SBP, the KASB bank withdrew its petition unconditionally. The offer of the Chinese company impacted the shares of the bank in the stock exchange in a positive way and doubled its share price.[26]

However, on 27 April, the KASB bank received a letter from the SBP titled "Draft Scheme of Amalgamation". The SBP used its powers, stated under section 47 of the Banking Companies Ordinance 1962. The section is stated earlier in this chapter. Despite the offer from a Chinese company that could be brought substantial foreign currency into the country, the SBP indulged in a controversial sale of the KASB to BankIslami.

The Public Accounts Committee (PAC), headed by the then chairman Syed Khurshid Shah, stated in a formal letter to the chief justice of Pakistan to take *suo motu* action to prevent the KASB bank from injustice.[27] The SBP provided

21 Ibid.

22 Asim Yasir, "Selling of KASB Bank to BI in Just RS 1000 Echoes in PAC Meeting", *International The News* (Pakistan, April 27, 2018).

23 Shahbaz Rana, "Legal Formalities of Defunct KASB Bank Remain Unfulfilled", *The Express Tribune* (Pakistan, September 08, 2019).

24 Ibid (Under the heading Not only the One).

25 Mian Abrar, "KASB Bank Merger – a Tale of Misplaced Priorities", *Pakistan Today* (May 09, 2015).

26 Shahbaz Rana, "Legal Formalities of Defunct KASB Bank Remain Unfulfilled", *The Express Tribune* (Pakistan, September 08, 2019).

27 Asim Yasir, "Selling of KASB Bank to BI in Just RS 1000 Echoes in PAC Meeting", *International The News* (Pakistan, April 27, 2018).

a loan of 15 billion PKR to the BankIslami for one year at 4.7 percent, in contrast to 7.6 percent, then a standard interest rate.[28] This resulted in a Rs 435 million loss to the national exchequer.[29] The PAC also asked the National Accountability Bureau (NAB) to initiate an inquiry in this matter. The NAB stated, in its preliminary report, that the SBP was unable to remain impartial in this sale and favoured the BankIslami in this deal.[30] The SBP not only failed to comply with its LOLR duties but also failed to maintain transparency in the sale of KASB Bank.

There was no dread concerning the solvency of the bank, which was functioning efficiently despite its failure to comply with MCR. Moreover, the bank was able to bring foreign investors to inject liquidity into KASB Bank, which was not the only beneficiary for the bank to meet the MCR but could impact positively on the financial system of Pakistan. That the CB of a country should act without any political influence is fine theoretically. Nonetheless, the decisions of the CB, even in developed countries, are arraigned for being politically influenced. Apparently, the KASB merger into BankIslami is a decision of the SBP followed by the failure of the bank to meet MCR. However, the former finance minister, who is in relegation to avoid the inquiries of embezzlement, is also accused of influencing this merger.[31] This was an unprecedented approach taken by a CB while acting as LOLR. The KASB could be rescued by injecting liquidity into it rather than providing a loan to BankIslami at a favoured rate of a mere 4.6 percent. The examples from the UK and the USA are, therefore, used to learn lessons to reform the regulatory framework in Pakistan. The examination of the case study of KASB Bank demonstrates that transparency in the operations of LOLR is more important than anything else.

## 4.2 Role of Financial Stability Board

In the modern era, financial stability becomes as imperative for the survival of a state as its defence. "Financial stability" means that an economic system is working smoothly. It has, thereby, emerged as one of the vital duties of the Central Bank of the country. The CB must intercept the vulnerability of its financial system and take preventive steps to ensure the trust of the investors.[32] The SBP is empowered under the State Bank of Pakistan Act, 1956 to act as a regulator for the financial system of Pakistan. SBP is obliged to

28 Mian Abrar, "KASB Bank Merger – a Tale of Misplaced Priorities", *Pakistan Today* (May 09, 2015).

29 Asim Yasir, "Selling of KASB Bank to BI in Just RS 1000 Echoes in PAC Meeting", *International The News* (Pakistan, April 27, 2018).

30 Ibid.

31 Mian Abrar, "KASB Bank Merger – a Tale of Misplaced Priorities", *Pakistan Today* (May 09, 2015).

32 https://www.sbp.org.pk/FS/4.4.asp

"regulate the monetary and credit system of Pakistan and to foster its growth in the best national interest".[33] Thereby, the SBP has established the Financial Stability Department (FSD) to ensure stability in the financial system country. SBP has also initiated working in many other areas aiming to ensure financial stability. It is now working on

a) Designing of financial stability framework.
b) Crisis management framework.
c) Review and update of consolidated supervision framework.
d) Framework for identification and supervision of D-SIP in Pakistan.

The SBP is also playing a vital role in ensuring the solvency of the individual financial institutions and in the smooth functioning of the payment system to make a hazard-free environment for the financial system of Pakistan. There is a Financial Stability Executive Committee (FSEC), which is an internal committee of the SBP is an official forum to discuss all the potential challenges to the financial system of Pakistan. FSEC is also empowered to take effective measures to maintain stability in the financial system. This committee is comprised of:

i) Governor, State Bank of Pakistan, is the Chair.
ii) Deputy Governor, Chief Economic Advisor, Executive Directors and Director FSD are members of this committee.[34]

This committee performs several vital duties to ensure stability in the financial system. It holds periodic assessments to intercept the potential challenges to the system. It also has a proper mechanism to monitor systemic risk. There is also a system of resolution framework which ensures a smooth settlement of the issues through a viable plan. This Board can be handy for the SBP while acting LOLR. Its reports and suggestions are based on empirical research; thereby, they are most likely to be correct. Nonetheless, in the case of KASB, the SBP didn't take input from FSEC. Resultantly, the SBP carried out a disputatious operation and allowed BankIslami to take over KASB Bank.[35]

KASB did not hold the position of the systemically important bank (SIB), like some other large banks working within the financial system of Pakistan. The powers of acting as LOLR are incorporated in the State Bank of Pakistan Act, 1956 through an amendment in 2015. There is no bank working in the financial system of Pakistan which was facing solvency challenges since then,

33 Ibid.
34 Ibid.
35 Mian Abrar, "KASB Bank Merger – a Tale of Misplaced Priorities", *Pakistan Today* (May 09, 2015).

nor has any such bank sought a rescue package from the SBP. It was only the KASB, in the recent past, which was taken over by the Islamic bank due to the challenges of solvency. Although, the SBP used its power of being a regulator vested under section 48 of the State Bank of Pakistan Act, 1956, and allowed another bank working in its financial system to take over KASB. Whereas the SBP was empowered to act as LOLR for KASB, thereby, the study of KASB, in spite of its status of not being a SIP, makes it consonant for this research.

## 4.3 Summary

This chapter provided a detailed argument on the problems which lie within the financial system of Pakistan and are causing serious financial troubles for the country. It argued on the establishment of the KASB Bank and its controversial amalgamation into the BankIslami. This chapter identified the problem of the financial system of Pakistan concerning the LOLR. It explained the capital requirement of the banking sector and argued that the SBP misused its regulatory powers in the case of KASB. This chapter highlights the key problems in the system. The reform proposal to address the issues identified in this chapter is provided in Chapter 6 of this research.

# 5 Appraisal of the Financial Systems of the UK, USA and Pakistan

This chapter of the research provides an insight into the system of LOLR in the UK and the US, and further, explicates the significance of this role to deter a financial crisis. This chapter is mainly divided into three parts. The first part examines the role of LOLR played by the SBP to identify the loopholes in the current regulation. Furthermore, it also discusses the role of the Bank of England as LOLR and the laws which empower the BOE to play this role. The second part of this chapter starts by arguing the establishment of the Federal Reserve Bank and elucidates the factors which compelled the policymakers to recognise the need for a CB. Moreover, it unfolds the essential characteristics of the Federal Reserve System and debates on the powers of FBR to play the role of LOLR before the Great Depression. This ends with a discussion of the legislative amendments which were made after the financial crisis of the 1930s and enhanced the powers of FBR as a LOLR. The third part consists of examples to illustrate the role of BOE and FBR as the LOLR. It further explains in detail the case of Northern Rock, Lehman Brothers, American Insurance Group, and enlightens on the principles which were used by the BOE and FBR while playing the role of LOLR. Furthermore, it compares the actions of BOE and FBR and describes the rules which they have followed. It derives certain lessons for the system of Pakistan which can be learned from the experiences of the UK and the US. Finally, this chapter concludes by providing a critical analysis of the role of LOLR played by the Federal Reserves, The Bank of England and the State Bank of Pakistan.

## 5.1 Comparison of the Systems of LOLR in the US and UK and Lending Lessons for Pakistan

The importance of LOLR has increased after the recent financial crisis, and it has become an essential part of the functions of CBs. The role of LOLR played by the Federal Reserves and Bank of England to deter the financial

DOI: 10.4324/9781003478768-5

crisis is widely venerated.[1] Although the unprecedented measures taken by the CBs of the countries have led to the emergence of LOLR, it has also raised several legislative issues and urged policy makers to regulate the operations of LOLR. In the modern economic system, the need for the LOLR cannot be denied, however; it requires a proper system to achieve the milestone of having a less vulnerable financial system.[2] Developing countries can take a lot from the examples of developed countries; nonetheless, it is not befitting to adopt policies from any financial system. There are numerous divergences in the dimensions of the economic systems and each economic system has its strengths and weaknesses.

Thus, no financial system can prosper by importing financial policies from developed countries because of the differences in the working of the systems. Notwithstanding, developing countries can learn lessons from them while keeping domestic needs in mind. Pakistan does not have a strong economy because of the absence of an efficient economic system. It is the need of the hour to implement robust policies; hence, Pakistan can learn many lessons from the systems of the United States and the United Kingdom. The rationale behind choosing these two systems lies in the similarities among the system of Pakistan, the US and the UK. Pakistan falls in commonwealth countries; therefore, the parable for the UK is befitting, and like the US, Pakistan also has potential in agriculture. To learn lessons from the US and UK, it is important to examine these systems and compare them to evaluate their strengths and loopholes.[3]

## 5.2 LOLR in the UK

Before 1871, Paris was the competitor of London in the international capital markets; nonetheless, the conquest of the French by the Prussians made London the sole centre of the international capital market. The establishment of the Bank of England played a vital role in the emergence of the domestic financial system. Leoni Levi argued that the CB is the LOLR in times of crisis. It is already discussed in part one of this research that CBs were reluctant to accept the responsibility of LOLR; however, by the 1870s, the BOE accepted this duty.[4] The Gurney Crisis and the principles regarding the role of LOLR

1 Marc Dobler, Simon Gray, Diarmuid Murphy, and Bozena Radzewicz-Bak, "The LOLR Function after the Global Financial Crisis" (2016) IMF Working Paper No. 16/10, ISBN: 9781498355995/1018-5941, Assessed: May 17, 2017.

2 Paul Tucker, "The LOLR and Modern Central Banking: Principles and Reconstruction" (2014) *Bank for International Settlement*, Page No. 10.

3 Dietrich Domanski, Richhild Moessner, and William R. Nelson, "CBs as LOLR: Experiences During the 2007–2010 Crisis and Lessons for the Future" (January 11, 2015) FEDS Working Paper No. 2014–110, Accessed: November 13, 2018.

4 Esther Madeleine Ogden, "The Development of the Role of the Bank of England as LOLR, 1870–1914" (September 1988) (Doctoral Thesis, City University London), Accessed: April 23, 2018.

by Bagehot, in his book *Lombard Street* in 1873, have played an important role in its emergence. The management of the money markets by the banking system of the UK is the key factor to make its position strong in the international sphere. It was then realised that the bank rate can be influential for the internal and external movement of the capital flow; hence, it will be effective to increase the reserves of the BOE. Initially, the bank rate strategy was used only during the crisis, but later, it was established that an effective bank rate policy will be befitting to protect the reserves.[5]

However, it did not work well and weakened the interaction between bank and market rates. The BOE made the discount houses more self-reliant in 1858, which consequently eroded their contact with the market. Secondly, the massive emergence of Joint Stock Banks (JSB) and the discount houses had affected the position of BOE as the "head of the financial system".[6] Lastly, in this period, the BOE was concerned about its income because JSBs were making more income. All these factors offered hindrance in the implementation of the bank rate policy.

In 1873, financial crisis started from the continent and swiftly spread across Europe and hit the market of the United States. The BOE was not affected by this crisis; hence, it had increased the bank rate, which helped a lot to gather massive reserves. The collapse of the City of Glasgow Bank in 1878 again created financial unrest. The BOE refused to rescue it because it was suspected that it was insolvent, which was later established by its failure. It was observed as a matter of fraud and mishandling; hence, its directors were tried and convicted, which had happened for the second time in the history of JSB in the United Kingdom.[7]

However, this case raised the contention against unlimited liabilities of the banking sector and hauled the system towards limited liabilities.[8] In that era, there were many bankruptcies in Scotland, and many financial institutions demanded help from the BOE, but there was no serious financial crisis. Due to many bankruptcies and financial issues during the 1870s, the BOE was able to attain full control over the bank rate and used it as an efficient tool to maintain its reserves. In 1890, the British financial system had faced another crisis, known as the Baring crisis, which mainly happened due to the loans of domestic and foreign financial institutions. The Baring Brothers have a long history of enriching the BOE to purchase gold from other CB and enhance its reserves, but the financial instability coerced them to seek a rescue operation

5 Ibid.

6 Ibid.

7 R. Button and S. Knott, "Desperate Adventurers and men of Straw: The Failure of City of Glasgow Bank and Its Enduring Impact on the UK Banking System" (Bank of England Publication, 2015), Accessed: April 24, 2018.

8 Esther Madeleine Ogden, "The Development of the Role of the Bank of England as LOLR, 1870–1914" (September 1988) *History, Economics, Business*, April 23, 2018.

from the BOE.[9] Afterward, the Baring crisis raised a major debate on how much liquidated reserves banks must keep all the time and to what extent they can depend on the support of the BOE.[10]

These financial crises, one after another, enhanced the need for a financial institution that could frame the financial policies of the country and provide liquidity support to the financial institutions facing problems. Sir Francis Baring, in 1797, argued that the financial system cannot survive without having a CB, and the CB must play the role of LOLR for the domestic market.[11] As it has already been discussed, financial institutions were individually lending liquidity in the form of loans, and the BOE also lent liquidity, but it was a loan against an interest rate. The BOE was also lending liquidity like the private institutions to earn profits; hence, the bank interest rate fluctuated to compete with market interest rate. Henry Thornton (1802) also emphasised the need for LOLR and expressed his concerns regarding the moral hazard problems (see Chapter 3).

In the nineteenth century, the British financial system faced several financial crises which exposed the vulnerability of the system and raised many questions.[12] Walter Bagehot (1873) analysed the financial system and located several reasons behind the financial crises. He made the skeleton of the operations of LOLR and argued that it could make a safe financial environment.[13] Although, there were many other domestic and international political and financial reasons which had caused the financial crisis, the main reason behind the collapse of the financial institutions was the escalation of panic among creditors. The presence of LOLR prevented the escalation of financial panic and strengthened the financial institutions against the crisis. Although Sir Francis Baring and Henry Thornton argued that the LOLR must be a vital part of the duties of the CB, it was badly disapproved due to the moral hazard problems by the policymakers.[14] Bagehot suggested that the CB must give its policy regarding the assistance of LOLR and lend freely to curtail the financial panic. It must only lend to the solvent financial institutions which can provide good collaterals. The issue of moral hazard can

9 Eugene N. White, "How to Prevent a Banking Panic: The Baring Crisis of 1890" (2016), <https://www.academia.edu/73436939/How_to_Prevent_a_Banking_Panic_the_Barings_Crisis_of_1890_Revisited>, Accessed: April 24, 2018.

10 Ibid.

11 Michael D. Bordo, "Rules for a Lender of Last Resort: An Historical Perspective" (2014) *Journal of Economic Dynamics and Control*, Vol. 49, Page No. 126.

12 David Laidler, "Two Views of the LOLR: Thornton and Bagehot" (2003), <https://economics.uwo.ca/people/laidler_docs/twoviews.pdf>, Accessed: April 24, 2018.

13 Vincent Bignon, Marc Flandreau, and Stefano Ugolini, "Bagehot for Beginners: The Making of LOLR Operations in the Mid-Nineteenth Century" (March 30, 2016), Accessed: April 24, 2018.

14 Mikko Niskanen, "Lender of Last Resort and the Moral Hazard Problem" (2002) Bank of Finland 17/2002, Accessed: August 10, 2017.

be addressed through a high penalty rate, which should be charged on the support of LOLR.[15]

The LOLR's functions have evolved with the progression of BOE as the CB of the State and played a vital role to prevent the system from the financial crisis. It was considered merely an operation of imparting liquidity during a crisis and was not considered as a continuous role to govern the financial system.[16] However, its operations played a vital role to extend its functions and achieve effective results. It was witnessed, during the crisis, that the financial institutions swiftly sold their assets, which caused deterioration in the value of those assets and made a more difficult situation. Thus, the BOE, while playing the role of LOLR, sometimes helped the financial institutions by purchasing their illiquid assets.[17] There are, nonetheless, many repercussions of these acts because of serious moral hazard issues which are discussed in Chapter 5.

During the twentieth century, the LOLR helped the financial system in tough times and prevented many crises. The last financial crisis occurred in 2007–08, in which the BOE used its discretionary powers, and at times, went beyond the principles of Bagehot.[18] Certain questions need to be addressed to make the role of LOLR more efficient. The principles of Bagehot emphasises that the LOLR support should only be for the illiquid but solvent financial institutions. However, it is quite difficult to identify the difference between illiquidity and insolvency. In the recent financial crisis, the role of LOLR is venerated, but its operational challenges have raised a debate to regulate it.[19]

In the modern financial system, where each country has many multinational countries, the role of LOLR is inseparable to curb the panic of a financial crisis and establish a less vulnerable system. Rather than being aloof from the financial system until the occurrence of financial unrest, the BOE is uninterruptedly playing the role of LOLR. It is important to remain in contact with the financial system to realise the need for the system and act rapidly to erode the panic of the crisis. The functions of LOLR have evolved in accordance with the needs of the financial system and are fully operating to establish a strong system. There are several cases in which the operations of LOLR helped the financial institutions to deter against crises like Baring Brother,

15 Vincent Bignon, Marc Flandreau, and Stefano Ugolini, "Bagehot for Beginners: The Making of LOLR Operations in the Mid-Nineteenth Century" (March 30, 2016), Accessed: April 24, 2018.

16 Paul Tucker, "The LOLR and Modern Central Banking: Principles and Reconstruction" (2014) *Bank for International Settlement*, Page No. 10.

17 Marc Dobler, Simon Gray, Diarmuid Murphy, and Bozena Radzewicz-Bak, "The LOLR Function after the Global Financial Crisis" (2016) IMF Working Paper No. 16/10, ISBN: 9781498355995/1018-5941, Assessed: May 17, 2017.

18 Vincent Bignon, Marc Flandreau, and Stefano Ugolini, "Bagehot for Beginners: The Making of LOLR Operations in the Mid-Nineteenth Century" (March 30, 2016), Accessed: April 24, 2018.

19 David Laidler, "Central Bank as the LOLR- Trendy or Passe" (University of Western Ontario, Economic Policy Research Institute 20048, 2004), Accessed: May 20, 2017.

Banking Sector of Scotland and Northern Rock.[20] It is befitting to evaluate the financial system of the US, as well, because it has a different historical background of the CB from that of the UK. The comparison of these systems will highlight the strengths and weaknesses of both systems and make it easy to learn worthy lessons for suggesting an appropriate regulatory framework of LOLR in Pakistan.

### *5.2.1 Legitimacy of LOLR in the United Kingdom*

The Bank of England was established in 1694 and was initially owned by private stakeholders. The BOE is the eighth-oldest bank in banking history and was nationalised in 1946.[21] Several countries esteemed it as a model while establishing their CB. The BOE is the only bank that emits new notes in England and Wales and is among one of the eight banks which are empowered to emit and regulate notes in the United Kingdom. The BOE is authorised to regulate the financial institutions working in the country and holds the power to set the interest rate for the banking system. The role of LOLR emerged as the role of the CB evolved in maintaining the stability of the financial system. Sir Francis Bearing, in his book *Observations on the Establishment of the Bank of England*, used the term "the dernier resort" for the CB. He argued that the CB must play the role of LOLR for the financial institutions which are facing liquidity shortage because, if no institution plays this role, a trivial panic regarding the financial crisis will be detrimental for the entire system. However, the problems of moral hazards were not addressed.[22]

After the financial crisis of 2007–2008, major reforms have been made to make a less vulnerable system. The Bank of England Act, 1998 states:

- The Bank of England is empowered to give monetary policy and give directions to the financial institutions which are carrying out their businesses within the jurisdiction of this Act.[23]
- The Bank of England is obliged to maintain price stability in the country by implementing the monetary policy and it should support the economic policies of the government.[24]

20 Mike Anson, David Bholat, Miao Kang, and Ryland Thomas, "The Bank of England as LOLR: New Historical Evidence from Daily Transactional Data" (November 2007) Staff Working Paper No. 691, Accessed: March 03, 2018.

21 John Plender, "On the Money: A History of the Bank of England", *Financial Times* (London, September 01, 2017).

22 Robert E. Keleher and Thomas M. Humphery, "The Lender of Last Resort a Historical Perspective" (1984) *Cato Journal*, Vol. 4, No. 1, Page No. 275.

23 The Bank of England Act, 1998, Section 10.

24 The Bank of England Act, 1998, Section 11(a)(b).

- Monetary Policy Committee should be constituted by the Bank of England, which must consist of the governor and deputy of the bank, two members must be appointed by the Governor after consultation of the Chancellor of the Exchequer, and four members should be appointed by the Chancellor of Exchequer. The committee will be responsible for formulating the monetary policy.[25]

The financial crisis of 2007–2008 became the reason for major changes in the regulations of the financial system. The Government decided to strengthen its financial system through new legislation aiming to address the loopholes in the financial laws. The Financial Services Act, 2012 was implemented. Resultantly, the Financial Policy Committee (FPC) and the Prudent Regulation Authority (PRA) were established to deal with financial stability. The role of the FPC is to identify the dread risks which can be detrimental to the stability of the financial system and take appropriate actions. The PRA plays the role of a regulator which regulates the commercial banks, building societies and investment firms that are carrying out their businesses in the UK.[26] The core aim of having a LOLR is to have an institution that ensures to take all necessary steps for making a prosperous financial system and protects the system from a financial crisis. Instead of leaving all the duties to deter a financial crisis on the CB, the BOE introduced a new method and opened new institutions that are performing certain duties that a LOLR should perform. However, BOE plays the role of surveillant for these institutions. In the financial system of the UK, there is no specific regulatory framework that governs the role of LOLR, but the system is developed by having more institutions. Notwithstanding, the BOE plays a vital part in the role of LOLR and lends liquidity to the commercial banks which suffer the problem of a liquidity shortfall. The presence of LOLR ensures the trust of the investors in the system and helps to deter a financial crisis. Northern Rock Bank was rescued by the BOE when it was experiencing the liquidity shortage through injecting liquidity into it.[27]

## 5.3 Central Banking in the United States

The history of LOLR started with the history of the CBs, which were established after realising that an institution that can regulate financial

25 The Bank of England Act, 1998, Section 13(1)(2).

26 Paul Tucker, "The LOLR and Modern Central Banking: Principles and Reconstruction" (2014) *Bank for International Settlement*, Page No. 10.

27 Marc Dobler, Simon Gray, Diarmuid Murphy, and Bozena Radzewicz-Bak, "The LOLR Function after the Global Financial Crisis" (2016) IMF Working Paper No. 16/10, ISBN: 9781498355995/1018-5941, Assessed: May 17, 2017.

institutions is inevitable. The emergence journey of the LOLR is extensively explicated in Chapter 1 of this research. However, to understand the role of LOLR in the jurisdiction of the United States, it is imperative to appraise the progression journey of the CB in the US. Usually, the Government owns the CB and empowers it, regulates the financial institutions and promotes the economic policies of the Government. Maintaining stability in the financial system is the utmost responsibility of a CB in the modern economic era. In 1791, the US Congress had declared the Bank of the United States as the CB bank. It was designed after learning lessons from the Bank of England. The establishment, unlike the BOE, was not welcomed by all the stakeholders, in general, and agrarians, in specific, had opposed the idea of having a CB and use of paper currency at the expense of gold and silver. The ownership of the bank was also disputed, and it was argued by many economists that the CB will favour the interests of commercial banks and industries.[28]

Although the foreign shareholders had no right to vote, which can influence the operations of the bank, still, it was a part of serious contentions that 70 percent of the shares were owned by foreigners till 1811.[29] The Bank of the United States (BUS) was obliged to perform its duties for both the public and private sectors. Disseminating the reserves in different parts of the country and controlling the supply of money through regulation was the most vigorous role of the BUS. It was privately owned and competing with other commercial banks to earn profit; hence, it faced major opposition because it had the right to regulate financial institutions at the same time it was competing with them. In 1811, at the renewal of the bank, it possessed 20 percent of the total national paper currency and was the most liquid bank in the US.[30] However, the constitutional objections, foreign ownership and public opinion regarding the bank led to its collapse, and it could not get a renewal from Congress and closed in 1811. The absence of the CB and its regulations allowed the commercial banks operating in the US to increase the number of banknotes. The absence of a regulator and race in emitting new notes caused inflation in 1812–1815, and prices for all commodities started increasing. The prices were increased at an average of 13.3 percent per year during that time. Deteriorating financial conditions evinced the significance of having a CB; hence, in 1815, the policymakers tried to establish a new CB but could not get consensus until 1816.[31]

28 David S. Kidwell and Richard Peterson, *Financial Institutions, Markets, and Money,* 5th edition (1993), Page No. 54, Dryden Press, 2000 - Business & Economics.

29 William F. Hixson, *Triumph of the Bankers: Money and Banking in the Eighteenth and Nineteenth Centuries* (Praeger, 1993), Page No. 115.

30 Edward L. Symons, Jr. and James J. White, *Banking Law,* 2nd edition (1984), Page No. 12.

31 John K. Galbraith, *Money: Whence It Came, Where It Went* (Houghton Mifflin, 1995), Page No. 13–58.

The Second Bank of the US was established in 1816 and was empowered with the same powers and assigned the same obligations as the first bank. The issue of foreign ownership was curtailed, and foreign ownership was reduced to 20 percent. The CB was obliged to maintain a currency principle to control inflation, but it could not capitalise on it. The legitimacy of the bank was challenged in the court, and the Supreme Court of the US decided, in McCulloch v. Maryland (1819), that the establishment of the Second Bank is constitutional. Chief Justice Marshall explicitly explicated that the act of establishing a CB is lawful and part of the supreme law of the State. The court reinforced its decision in the case of Osborn v. Bank of the United States (1824).[32] The Second Bank of the US was able to gain some control over the money supply and managed to maintain financial stability until 1828. Congress produced a bill for the renewal of the bank in 1832 and voted for it. However, President Jackson used his veto powers and rejected the bill of renewal of the Second Bank of the US. Thus, the Second Bank of the United States became dysfunctional in 1836, when its charter expired.

After a long gap, the National Banking Acts of 1863 and 1864 were framed to implement the economic policies of the federal government on the banking system instead of establishing a new CB. The main purpose of implementing these acts was:

a) Establish a system for the national banks.
b) Recognise one national currency.
c) Create a secondary market for treasury resources.[33]

Although the National Banking Acts played a vital role in regulating the banking system of the US, they were unable to address the issues of inelastic currency and liquidity. The small banks in the rural areas were having their deposits in large, urban banks. The rural banks require their liquidity in the planting season and the urban banks used their deposits in autumn. The larger banks had tried to fulfil the liquidity demand of the small rural banks but could not maintain it for long. Consequently, in 1873, 1884, 1893 and the wall street panic of 1907, the financial system of the US had faced financial crises.[34]

The Federal Reserve Act, 1913 was a major milestone in the history of the CB in the US, which initially proposed a new model for the banking system. A Federal Reserve System was established, which was owned by private banks and operated in the interest of the public. Bankers could run 12 banks;

32 William F. Hixson, *Triumph of the Bankers: Money and Banking in the Eighteenth and Nineteenth Centuries* (Praeger, 1993), Page No. 117.

33 Ibid, Page No. 120–50.

34 Barry P. Bosworth and Aaron Flaaen, "America's Financial Crisis: The End of an Era", *Brooking* (April 14, 2009), Accessed: November 05, 2018.

however, those banks were supervised by the Federal Reserve Board, consisting of the members of the Secretary of the Treasury, the Comptroller of the Currency and other officials which the President can appoint. The Federal Reserve System was amended twice after the Great Depression and a financial crisis of the 1970s to address the loopholes. The Federal Reserve Bank of the US consists of 12 regional banks and plays the role of CB for the US. It was established under the Federal Reserve System, which was framed in the Federal Reserve Act 1913. All 12 regional banks are jointly responsible to implement the monetary policy of the federal government. The system of central banking in the US is different from many other systems because the countries normally have one institution as the CB, but in the US, 12 banks are operating as the CB under Federal Reserve System.[35]

### *5.3.1 LOLR in the US*

The US has recognised the need for the role of LOLR to address the panic regarding the collapse of the financial system after a deliberate examination of financial crises. No financial system can survive without reserving the trust of its investors because, if the investors feel unsafe in an economic environment, they will withdraw their money. The liquidity shortage of a financial institution can be addressed by selling illiquid assets or borrowing money from an institution that has the capacity to lend. However, if panic regarding the system surges among the depositors, it increases the demand for liquidity, which makes it nearly impossible for the financial institution to survive. Thus, the intervention of LOLR is paramount for a financial system to survive financial panic. The Great Depression and the recent financial crisis of 2007–2008 elucidated how much perilous financial panic among the depositors can be for a financial system.[36]

A deliberate appraisal of the failure of the banking system divulges that there are two major factors that can lead to its collapse. The first factor is internal, which is mismanagement, dishonesty and concealment of facts; and the second is external, which includes changes in relative prices and major changes in overall prices. The changes in relative prices can affect the value of the banking assets immensely. However, an astute banking structure can prevent the failure of the banking system caused by the changes in relative prices. A banking system that allows the banks to have nationwide branches can absorb the effects caused by the changes in relative prices. In the 1920s,

35 The Federal Reserve System: Purposes & Function (Federal Reserve System Publications), Last Updated October 25, 2018, <https://www.federalreserve.gov/aboutthefed/files/pf_1.pdf>, Accessed: November 05, 2018.

36 Stanley Fischer, "The Lender of Last Resort Function in the United States" (2016) *International Finance*, Vol. 2, Page No. 239–60.

nearly 6,000 banks collapsed which were operating in the small agriculture unit. Nonetheless, in Canada, where the banking structure was different, the banks having nationwide branches remained persistent, and no bank was closed. Additionally, several branches of the banks were closed which were operating in the small regions.[37] In elucidating the significance of the role of LOLR, Friedman and Schwartz argued that, had the Federal Reserve Bank acted in a timely manner as LOLR and injected the required amount of liquidity into the financial market in 1930 and 1931, the deteriorating value of the banking assets could have been avoided.[38]

A financial system must have a CB which can implement monetary policies of the government and regulate the financial institutions. The strength of a financial system always lies in the trust which its depositors have in it; however, it is not surprising that a financial institution starts experiencing liquidity problems. Thus, the presence of an institution that can lend liquidity during a financial panic is inevitable, and this is one of the main reasons behind the establishment of the Federal Reserve Bank so that it can play the role of LOLR for the financial institutions operating in the US.[39] The LOLR can protect the financial system and help to keep the interest of the investors. However, bad policies for operation of this role and a continuous dependency of the financial institutions on its facilities can make it a cause of a major financial crisis.

FBR played an important role as a LOLR to overcome the damages of financial crises which occurred at different times. The acumen behind having a LOLR is to maintain stability in the financial system; that is why, in 2007–2009, the FBR reduced its interest rate and lent liquidity to financial institutions. The rationale behind reducing the interest rate was to encourage investment and maintain stability in the financial system. Thus, FBR has reduced its interest rate from 5.25 percent to 0–0.25 percent.[40] However, mere the policy of lowering the interest rate was not enough to address the problem of the financial crisis because the commercial banks were illiquid and facing the problems of insolvency. A major deflation occurred in the prices of all illiquid assets of the financial institutions which had turned the situation into a crisis. The anxiety of the financial crisis urged CBs around the globe to take unprecedented steps. Therefore, even the BOE superseded the principle of

37 Michael D. Bordo, "The LOLR. Some Historical Insights" (1989) *Proceeding Federal Reserve Bank of Chicago*, Page No. 177–97.

38 Ibid.

39 Stanley Fischer, "The Lender of Last Resort Function in the United States" (2016) *International Finance*, Vol. 2, Page No. 239–60.

40 Hansjörg Herr, Sina Rüdiger, and Jennifer Pédussel Wu, "The Federal Reserve as LOLR During Subprime Crisis- Successful Stabilization Without Structural Changes" (2016) Institute for International Political Economy Berlin, Working Paper No. 65/2016, Accessed: November 07, 2018.

Walter Bagehot to lend against good collateral because it is very difficult to evaluate if the collateral is sound or not, especially during a crisis. Therefore, the FBR injected $1.2 trillion into the private sector, aiming to maintain the stability of the financial system against the crisis.[41]

The financial system of the US was governed without having a CB before the formation of the Federal Reserve System. Initially, many economists were against the presence of LOLR due to the moral hazard problems pertaining to it. However, the evolution of the banking system and a deep study of financial crises revealed the needs of a financial system. The banking system of the US faced collapses of many banks; however, the establishment of the CB and its role as a LOLR to control the effects of crises is appreciated. Before the occurrence of the financial crisis of 2007–2008, the role of LOLR was not properly legislated in the US like in other countries.[42] The FBR played the role of LOLR and used its discretionary powers in recusing the financial institutions. A deliberate examination of the operations of FBR enunciates that no hard and fast rule was deployed to carry out rescue operations. The acumen behind the presence of a LOLR is to strengthen the financial system against crisis, and the CBs are empowered to take all necessary steps to ensure the stability of the financial system.[43]

The FBR hasn't restricted itself to the principles of Walter Bagehot that the CB should lend freely, but only to the institutions which are solvent and susceptible to provide worthy collateral. Additionally, the CB must charge a high-interest rate and make this clear ahead of the financial crisis, on which ground the CB will intervene and rescue the financial institutions. Instead, the FBR reduced its interest rate during the crisis and lent liquidity without bothering about the market value of the available collaterals. Thus, all the efforts of FBR were unhandy to deter the financial crisis; nonetheless, it was able to minimise the damage. The liquidity was injected into the financial system to curtail the dread of the investors, which is a core function of the role of LOLR. However, the FBR failed to enforce its policies appropriately, which is also an integral part of LOLR because, without implementing the financial policies regarding the assistance of LOLR, it will itself turn out to be a major cause of the crisis.[44] The ignorance of the moral hazard problems and continuous

41 Stanley Fischer, "The Lender of Last Resort Function in the United States" (2016), *International Finance*, Vol. 2, Page No. 239–60.

42 Michael D. Bordo, "The LOLR: Some Historical Insights" (1989) *Proceeding Federal Reserve Bank of Chicago*, Page No. 177–97.

43 Kenneth N. Kuttner, "The Federal Reserve as LOLR during the Panic of 2008" (Department of Economics, Williams Collage, December 30, 2008), Accessed: November 09, 2018.

44 Hansjörg Herr, Sina Rüdiger, and Jennifer Pédussel Wu, "The Federal Reserve as LOLR During Subprime Crisis- Successful Stabilization Without Structural Changes" (2016) Institute for International Political Economy Berlin, Working Paper No. 65/2016, Accessed: November 07, 2018.

lending of liquidity is more detrimental than the collapse of a financial institution. The conception of moral hazard problems is extensively explicated in Chapter 1 of this research.

### *5.3.2 Legitimacy of LOLR in the US*

After the inception of the banking sector in the economic system at a domestic and international level, the growth of the financial system became faster. Banks obtain money from depositors, who have a surplus and offer them interest for their deposits and lend it to the debtors and charge interest from them. This made it easy for financial institutions and even for individuals to obtain debt and invest in their businesses. Doing business has become much easier in the presence of the banking sector than it was ever before. Although, mainly, banks provide loans to their customers and charge interest, other financial institutions and even natural persons who are susceptible to lend liquidity are also lending liquidity on personal relations or mutually understood stipulations. The financial institutions in the modern economic era are dependent on each other, especially on banks, to fulfil the problems of liquidity. However, in the anxiety of financial unrest, banks sometimes face liquidity shortages to fulfil the demand for liquidity, or in some cases, they are reluctant to lend liquidity due to uncertain financial situations.[45]

Banks are providing tremendous services to financial institutions and contributing a lot to the economic growth of domestic and international systems. However, the avarice of earning more dragged them into the involvement of risky financial activities, which, consequently, became a major cause of financial crises. The economic system of the US was governed for many decades without a CB; nonetheless, the role of the CBs like BOE to handle the economic system against financial crises compelled the policymakers in the US to recognise the need for a CB. Furthermore, new banking regulation in the form of the Basel Accord, which imposes certain obligations on the banking industries and requires them to maintain a minimum capital, is strengthening the financial system around the globe.[46]

It was the time when the conception of having monetary policy was not invented. The financial panic of 1907 could be easily addressed by the presence of LOLR, which could lend liquidity to the financial institutions which were

45 Gary Gorton and Andrew Metrick, "The Federal Reserve and Panic Prevention: The Roles of Financial Regulation and LOLR" (2013) *The Journal of Economic Perspectives*, Vol. 27, No. 4, Page No. 45–64.

46 Ellis W. Tallman and Elmus Wicker, "Banking and Financial Crises in United States History: What Guidance Can History Offer Policymakers?" (August 2010) FBR of Cleveland Working Paper No. 10–09, Accessed: November 07, 2018.

enduring the liquidity shortfall. Thus, FRB was established to play the role of LOLR for the financial system of the US and ensures the trust of the investors in the system. The FBR played an admirable role and deterred seasonal financial panics. However, its failure to protect the financial system from the detrimental effects of the great depression in the 1930s raised several questions on its capability to protect the system from the financial crisis. The Federal Reserve Act, 1913 has established the FBR and empowers it with certain authorities.[47]

- The Reserve Bank Committee (RBC) was established, which consisted of the Secretary of the Treasury, the Comptroller of the Currency and the Secretary of Agriculture, which was mandated to establish Federal Reserve Cities not less than eight or more than 12. The RBC shall divide the United States into districts, and no district shall contain more than one federal reserve city. The district can be readjusted or more districts can be created by the Federal Reserve Board; however, the maximum number of districts can be 12.[48]
- The RBC holds the power to seek assistance from expert counsel where it is deemed necessary. Each district shall have a Federal Reserve Bank and the RBC shall supervise everything to establish reserve banks in the districts. The Federal Reserve Bank shall include the name of the city in which it is established for example "The Federal Reserve Bank of Chicago".[49]
- Each Federal Reserve Bank constituted under the Federal Reserve Act by the RBC shall open its branches within the district in which the federal reserve bank is located. It is also empowered to open its branches in another district where the federal reserve bank has been suspended under section 2 of the federal reserve act, 1913.[50]
- The branches of the Federal Reserve Banks shall be operated by the board directors under the rules and regulations approved by the Federal Reserve Board. The directors of these branches shall not be less qualified than the directors of the Federal Reserve Bank. The bank is empowered to appoint four directors in these branches, and three directors shall be appointed by the Federal Reserve Board. All these directors will remain in their offices for the time the directors of the Federal Reserve Bank and Federal Reserve Board will. The Federal Reserve Bank shall appoint one of the directors as the manager of the branch.[51]
- After the establishment of the federal reserve cities by the FRC under section two of the Federal Reserve Act, 1913 the handler of the currency shall

47 Benjamin Remy Chabot, "The Federal Reserve's Evolving Monetary Policy Implementation Framework: 1914–1923" (January 19, 2017) FBR of Chicago Working Paper No. WP-2017–1, Accessed: November 07, 2018.

48 The Federal Reserve Act, 1913, Section 2.

49 Ibid.

50 The Federal Reserve Act, 1913, Section 3.

51 Ibid.

issue a certificate stating the geographical jurisdiction of each Federal Reserve Bank.[52]

- The Federal Reserve Board shall consist of seven members, five of which shall be appointed by the President of the US after the consent of the Senate and Secretary of the Treasury and the manager of the currency shall also be the ex officio members. All these five members appointed by the President shall be from five different federal reserve districts.[53]
- The members of the Federal Reserve Board during the term in their office and after two years shall not be eligible to work in any Federal Reserve Bank. Furthermore, two out of the five members appointed by the President shall be experienced in the field of banking or finance.[54]
- Each Federal Reserve Bank is empowered to lend liquidity to the banking sectors which is working within its geographical jurisdiction if that bank can provide worthy collaterals and shall charge a high-interest rate on its lending to discourage the dependency of the banking system on the Federal Reserve Bank.[55] The banking institutions can seek liquidity assistance from the Federal Reserve Bank when they are facing a liquidity shortfall and no other financial institution is willing to lend them. However, it is explicitly stated in the Act that lending liquidity is a discretionary power of the Federal Reserve Bank.

The Federal Reserve Banks performed well, in contrast to the performance of the first and second CB of the US. However, the Great Depression started a new debate on the capacity of the Federal Reserve Banks. A deliberate evaluation of the causes of the Great Depression and the limitation of the Federal Reserve Banks in addressing the financial issues revealed that the conditions to lend liquidity to the banking sector were very strict. Thus, the Federal Reserve Act, 1913 was amended and the lending powers of the FRBs were greatly expanded. In 1932, section 13.3 was added to the Act, which waived certain obligations to lend liquidity and allowed the FRBs to lend liquidity not only to the banks but to nonbanks and private sectors. The strictness of providing worthy collaterals was also loosened. The growth of financial and banking sectors created several new challenges for Federal Reserve Banks; thus, the banks were granted more powers to address the issue and protect the system from financial crises. Monetary Control Act, 1980 and Federal Deposit Insurance Corporation Improvement Act, 1991 further allowed the Federal Reserve Banks to lend liquidity to the financial institutions when they need it.[56]

52 The Federal Reserve Act, 1913, Section 4.

53 The Federal Reserve Act, 1913, Section 10.

54 Ibid.

55 The Federal Reserve Act, 1913, Section 13.

56 Hansjörg Herr, Sina Rüdiger, and Jennifer Pédussel Wu, "The Federal Reserve as LOLR During Subprime Crisis- Successful Stabilization Without Structural Changes" (2016) Institute for International Political Economy Berlin, Working Paper No. 65/2016, Accessed: November 07, 2018.

The vast powers of the FRBs to lend liquidity to the banks and nonbanks could not prevent the financial system of the US from the financial crisis of 2007–2008. It was argued by many economists that the ability of FRBs to lend liquidity even if the financial institution or the commercial banks seeking the liquidity were unable to provide worthy collaterals caused a financial crisis. The role of LOLR is good for the financial system; however, a continuous dependency of the financial institutions on the liquidity support of the LOLR can harm the entire system. The Dodd-Frank Act, 2010 was framed after the recent financial crisis to impose certain restrictions on the discretionary powers of the FRBs to lend liquidity. The purpose of implementing the Dodd-Frank Act, 2010 is to reduce the need for LOLR.[57] Although certain restrictions are imposed on the facility of LOLR by the Dodd-Frank Act, still, the FRBs are empowered to act as LOLR in different ways. The FRBs can provide discount window loans to depository institutions, commercial banks, credit unions, thrift institutions and foreign banks instead of directly lending liquidity. Such loans can be provided to individual institutions that are facing problems or to the banking sector to deter the stress of the crisis.[58] The Dodd-Frank Act, 2010 has not restricted the FRBs from playing the role of LOLR but imposes some conditions; it requires the banks to publish the information regarding the discount windows and the details of the debtors. Walter Bagehot's rule to lend liquidity freely but only to the institutions which can provide good collaterals is reinforced through the Dodd-Frank Act, 2010.[59]

## 5.4 Comparison of the Systems of LOLR in UK and US

The banking system of the UK is one of the oldest and most developed systems in the world. Many countries have used this system as a model while establishing their banking system. The banking system, due to its contribution to the evolution of societies and economic systems, has turned out to be an integral part of the financial system. The conception of borrowing money for business or personal purposes is far older than the history of banking. However, lending and borrowing were merely based on personal relations, and the conditions varied from case to case. A person, legal or natural, could only obtain debts on his acquaintances, which was providing opportunities only for a smaller part

57 W. J. Dodwell, "Reforms of the Dodd-Frank Act and Its Implication" (2016–2017) *Review of Banking & Financial Law*, Vol. 36, Accessed: November 10, 2018.

58 Gary Gorton and Andrew Metrick, "The Federal Reserve and Panic Prevention: The Roles of Financial Regulation and LOLR" (2013) *The Journal of Economic Perspectives*, Vol. 27, No. 4, Page No. 45–64.

59 Stanley Fischer, "The Lender of Last Resort Function in the United States" (2016) *International Finance*, Vol. 2, Page No. 239–60.

of the society,[60] although the beginning of the banking system was not much different than the pre-banking rituals because banks were mainly owned by private individuals and they offered loans on personal relations. Due to the significance and input of the banking system in the financial system, serious contentions were originated regarding its capacity and rules of businesses. It was recognised that the banking system can only continue to perform well if it will be properly regulated. Thus, the conception of a CB was invented which can regulate the banking system and play the role of a surveillant. The concept of having a LOLR was also an imperative element in establishing a CB.[61]

In the UK, the banking system was warmly accepted because of its services and input in the growth of national income. The banks started their business by obtaining deposits on a relatively lower interest rate and lent it to the borrowers at a higher rate for business purposes in the beginning, and for personal matters, too, afterward. Banks became a trustworthy institution for the deposition of saving and getting interest as well. The acumen behind operating a banking system is to earn money; therefore, many commercial banks started to get involved in risky but profitable ventures. The loopholes in the banking regulations were fully used by the banking system for their interests. Eventually, after a tremendous start due to insured loans and the failure of the debtors to return money, banking sectors around the world started collapsing.[62]

The policymakers had concluded that there must be a CB in each financial system that shall regulate the banking system while understanding the needs of the system. The BOE was a private bank and was carrying out its operations to earn money; hence, its ability to work as a regulator was questioned while remaining a competitor in the market. The role of LOLR is also older than the history of CB, but this was also played based on personal relations. Not only banks but the financial institutions were helping each other in difficult times by lending liquidity. However, these lending operations were purely based on mutual understandings, but it was recognised, after the collapse of several banks, that the system cannot be governed without having an official LOLR. The CB, which holds several powers to regulate the system and emit new notes, was also assigned with the duty of playing the role of LOLR for the financial institutions which were facing financial problems.[63]

60 Neslihan Dincbas, Tomasz Kamil Michalski, and Evren Ors, "Banking Integration and Growth: Role of Banks' Previous Industry Exposure" (July 21, 2017) HEC Paris Research Paper No. FIN-2015-1096, Accessed: October 05, 2018.

61 Heidi Mandanis Schooner, "CBs' Role in Bank Supervision in the United States and United Kingdom" (January 2003) *Brooklyn International Law Journal*, Vol. 28, Issue (2), Page No. 5–25. Accessed: October 06, 2018.

62 Marc Flandreau and Stefano Ugolini, "Where It All Began: Lending of Last Resort and the Bank of England During the Overend-Gurney Panic of 1866" (May 27, 2011) Norges Bank Working Paper No. 2011/03, Accessed: August 11, 2018.

63 Michael Anson, David Bholat, Miao Kang, and Ryland Thomas, "The Bank of England as LOLR: New Historical Evidence from Daily Transaction Date" (November 17, 2017) Bank of England Working Paper No. 691, Accessed: March 03, 2018.

On the other hand, in the US right after its independence, the first CB was established in 1791, which was empowered to regulate the financial market. In the US, the concept of having a CB was not warmly accepted because it was a bank not only owned by private individuals, but nearly 40 percent of shareholders were foreigners. The banking system of the US is different from the system of the UK because, unlike the UK's banks, which lent to the financial institutions, the US banks were lending to the agriculture industry. The first CB of the US was also mandated to lend liquidity to the banks which were facing liquidity shortfall. However, even after lending liquidity to many banks, the CB was not able to protect against the collapse of banks. After its failure, the second CB was established in 1816; however, unfortunately, nearly 20 percent of shares of this bank were also owned by foreigners. The second CB of the US was also established to strengthen the system not only with regulations but also through lending liquidity to the banks that were facing problems. The second CB of the US was not backed by the politicians; that is why, eventually, it also failed and was abolished in 1836.[64]

The US banking system was governed without a CB for more than 70 years before the establishment of the Federal Reserve Bank in 1913. The banking collapse in the US was more severe than any other competitive country in the nineteenth century. After a long debate, the policymakers of the US had concluded that the banking system cannot survive without having a LOLR which can ensure the trust of the investors and lend liquidity to the banks which are merely illiquid not insolvent and can be protected through injecting liquidity.[65] A Federal Reserve System (FRS) was established under the Federal Reserve Act, 1913, which was mandated to establish a CB for the US. The banking system of the US is very diverse and big, as compared to the banking system of the UK. The FRS has divided the United States of America into 12 parts and has established 12 banks that are empowered to operate as the CB of the US. A frequent dependency of the financial institutions on it can harm the system even more severely than the collapse of an institution.[66]

The FRB was established mainly to regulate the banking system of the US and lend liquidity to the banks to protect them from collapsing. Section 13 of the Federal Reserve Act, 1913 empowers the FRB to act as the LOLR for the banking sector in case of a financial crisis. The framework, which was framed by Walter Bagehot, was adopted to empower the FRB for playing the role of

64 Barry P. Bosworth and Aaron Flaaen, "America's Financial Crisis: The End of an Era", *Brooking* (April 14, 2009), Accessed: November 05, 2018.

65 David S. Kidwell and Richard Peterson, *Financial Institutions, Markets, and Money,* 5th edition (1993), Page No. 54. The Dryden Press Series in Finance.

66 Vincent Bignon, Marc Flandreau, and Stefano Ugolini, "Bagehot for Beginners: The Making of LOLR Operations in the Mid-Nineteenth Century" (March 30, 2016), Accessed: April 24, 2018.

LOLR. The FRB played its role admirably and curtailed sessional financial panics until the Great Depression. The FBR was allowed to lend liquidity only to the banks on the grounds if they can provide good collateral. However, after the Great Depression, the Federal Reserve Act, 1913 was amended and section 13.3 was added to it. The FRB was authorised to lend liquidity to the nonbanks and private sector which required liquidity assistance. The requirement of producing worthy collaterals for getting liquidity support was also loosened. The FRB played the role of LOLR effectively for many financial institutions and protected them from collapsing after getting a mandate to lend freely.[67]

The BOE has played a vital role in maintaining the stability of the financial institutions operating in the UK in the recent financial crisis of 2007–2008. The BOE lends liquidity to many financial institutions, and on many occasions, it bought the illiquid assets of the financial institutions to curtail the panic regarding the collapse of the institution and thereby ensured the trust of the investors in the system. The BOE superseded the principles proposed by Walter Bagehot for the role of LOLR and lent to some financial institutions without demanding good collaterals.[68] The unprecedented role of the BOE in lending liquidity helped the financial institutions to survive the financial crisis. Notwithstanding, many institutions were refused to be rescued by the BOE because the bank was of the opinion that those financial institutions were insolvent, and injecting liquidity will not help to protect them. The BOE still enjoys several discretionary powers in playing the role of LOLR because no restrictions are being imposed on its powers so far.[69]

The Federal Reserve Bank played a vigorous role as a LOLR to protect financial institutions from collapsing in the recent financial crisis of 2007–2008. The FRB implements the monetary policy of the State on its financial institutions. To ensure the trust of the investors, the FRB injected $1.2 trillion into the financial system and lent to the financial institutions which were not capable of providing good collateral. However, unlike the BOE, the discretionary powers of FRB are amended after the financial crisis through the Dodd-Frank Act, 2010. Although the powers of FRB were amended after the financial crisis, still, the role of LOLR played by the bank in curbing the effects of the crisis is recognised. The significance of the role of LOLR is

67 Hansjörg Herr, Sina Rüdiger, and Jennifer Pédussel Wu, "The Federal Reserve as LOLR During Subprime Crisis- Successful Stabilization Without Structural Changes" (2016) Institute for International Political Economy Berlin, Working Paper No. 65/2016, Accessed: November 07, 2018.

68 Paul Tucker, "The LOLR and Modern Central Banking: Principles and Reconstruction" (2014) *Bank for International Settlement*, Page No. 10.

69 Paul Tucker, "The LOLR and Modern Central Banking: Principles and Reconstruction" (2014) BIS Paper No. 79, Accessed: February 03, 2018.

accepted, and to make it more efficient, it is further regulated to maintain stability in the financial system.[70]

## 5.5 Examples of the LOLR Operations from the UK and USA

The essential characteristics of LOLR can be illustrated by the evaluation of the rescue operations conducted by the CBs in different eras and jurisdictions. LOLR is not an institution that is assigned the duty to lend liquidity during a financial crisis, nor does it have a mere duty to impart liquidity to the financial institutions which are experiencing a shortfall in liquidity. Among many other duties of CBs, LOLR is also a vital part. Examples of the UK and USA unveil the progression of this role, which started from injecting liquidity into the financial system in times of financial panic and has turned out to be an indispensable part to govern the economic system.[71] The LOLR ensures the trust of investors in the system by injecting liquidity, buying illiquid assets of financial institutions and regulating the financial system. The Bank of England and Federal Reserve Bank played the role of LOLR for financial institutions to deter the financial crises at different times. The fruitful outcomes of this role made it an integral part of the system and obliterated the contentions that the presence of LOLR is detrimental for the system due to the moral hazard problems pertaining to it.[72]

The Bank of England has played an imperative role as LOLR to strengthen financial institutions during the financial crises of 1847, 1857 and 1866. The role which the BOE has played was not based on the principles framed by Henry Thornton and Walter Bagehot. The BOE dealt with the crises on the basis of the reasons behind it and lent liquidity to financial institutions, which varied from case to case. Initially, the BOE had only provided liquidity assistance to its top borrowers instead of injecting it into the system. It can be examined that many financial institutions were rescued without even demanding the collateral. The principle of charging a high-interest rate was followed in the crises of 1857 and 1866. However, it was superseded in the crisis of 1847.[73]

The role of LOLR played by the BOE was criticised by many economists, who argued that there must be a similar approach for all financial institutions

70 W. J. Dodwell, "Reforms of the Dodd-Frank Act and Its Implication" (2017) *Review of Banking & Financial Law*, Vol. 36, Page No. 21.

71 Dietrich Domanski, Richhild Moessner, and William R. Nelson, "CBs as LOLR: Experiences During the 2007–2010 Crisis and Lessons for the Future" (January 11, 2015) FEDS Working Paper No. 2014–110, Accessed: November 13, 2018.

72 Ibid.

73 Michael Anson, David Bholat, Miao Kang, and Ryland Thomas, "The Bank of England as LOLR: New Historical Evidence from Daily Transaction Date" (November 17, 2017) Bank of England Working Paper No. 691, Accessed: March 03, 2018.

while acting as LOLR. Otherwise, this facility will only remain between the bank and its favourite customers. The presence of LOLR faced criticism due to the moral hazard problems relating to it. Thus, the BOE had used multiple approaches to curb the effects of moral hazard problems. A thorough study of the role of BOE as LOLR imparts that the principles of Walter Bagehot were used in many incidents but not strictly followed all the time. Many financial institutions were not rescued because the directors of the BOE were of the opinion that those institutions were insolvent. The role of LOLR during the financial crisis of 2007–2008 has played a vital role in its progression.[74]

### *5.5.1 Northern Rock's Run*

From 14 September to 17 September, Northern Rock was the first bank to run due to the liquidity crisis in the United Kingdom since Victorian times.[75] The directors of Northern Rock were responsible for the difficulties that the company has faced since August 2007. A reckless business model was pursued by the directors, who were mainly reliant on wholesale fundings. It was the regulatory failure of the Financial Service Authority to ensure that Northern Rock did not pose a systematic risk.[76] The Chancellor of the Exchequer reported that the concerned bank is posing a systematic risk to the financial system, and thereby, immediately authorised the BOE to intervene. However, the tripartite authorities failed to materialise an adequate support plan by not announcing the Government's guarantee on the deposits of the Rocks.[77] Northern Rock had 4,811 full-time and 1,125 part-time employees at the end of 2006.[78] It was formerly building security; nonetheless, it was demutualised on 1 October 1997. It had assets of £101 billion by the end of 2006.[79] In the Community Report, it has described itself as "a specialist lender"; thereby, 89.2 percent of its assets were residential mortgages.[80]

On 9 August 2007, due to the global shock to the financial system in which the American sub-prime mortgage was the one burnt badly, the banks' traders noted a "dislocation in the market" for their funds. The worldwide liquidity crisis surprised Northern Rock as well. They were expecting to maintain the attraction of funds by using their low-risk mortgages but failed to do so. It could not foresee the closing of its financial markets simultaneously. It had

74 Chris Giles, "Bank of England Defends Response to Financial Crisis after Criticism", *Financial Times Economics Editor* (April 10, 2018), Accessed: November 13, 2018.

75 HC Deb, January 26, 2008, Vol. 1. (House of Commons Treasury Committee, The Run on the Rocks, fifth Report of Session 2007–2008).

76 HC Deb, January 26, 2008, Vol. 1.

77 Ibid.

78 Northern Rock, Annual Report 2006, Page No. 72.

79 Ibid, Page No. 59.

80 Ibid, Page No. 9 & 82.

its funding programmes in the United States, Europe, Far East, Canada and Australia; thereby, its administration was careless because it was unlikely that all of the markets will close simultaneously.[81] The Governor of the BOE stated that Northern Rock did not bother to have insurance against any potential trouble and referred to a bank of the United States countrywide that, too, had faced liquidity crisis due to the US's sub-prime crisis. It had paid millions of dollars for its liquidity insurance; therefore, it was able to claim that insurance during the crisis and maintained to draw down $11.5 billion of committed credit lines.[82]

In the case of Northern Rock, the BOE has used an approach of nationalisation of the institution to avoid the effects of moral hazard problems. It sometimes becomes difficult for the CB to refuse liquidity assistance to a financial institution, even if the institution is insolvent and unable to provide worthy collateral. Thus, the CBs use their discretionary powers and rescue such institutions because they have an immense impact on the system, and their collapse can deeply harm the entire system. The acumen behind having a LOLR is not to protect the institutions which are facing liquidity challenges but to protect the system; and for that purpose, the CBs protect the institutions.[83] That is why the BOE did not provide free liquidity to Northern Rock. There is a regulatory failure, as well, in the collapse of the concerned bank. The Financial Services Authority has acknowledged that the business model of Northern Rock was clearly indicating the risks associated with it. Rapid growth as a company and a fall in its share price since February 2007 were the clear signs of high risk. However, as a regulator, the FSA failed to tackle the basic impediments in its funding model and did nothing to prevent the problems.[84]

The bank of Northern Rock started facing liquidity problems, and its failure could escalate the detrimental effects of the financial crisis of 2007–2008. The bank tried to fulfil the demand for liquidity through the sale of its illiquid assets; however, the anxiety of financial crisis and panic among the investors made it difficult for it to survive. The moral hazard problems have remained in the debates since the inception of LOLR, and many economists have proposed several methods to curtail the effects of moral hazard problems.[85] The CB

81 HC Deb, January 26, 2008, Vol. 1. (House of Commons Treasury Committee, The Run on the Rocks, fifth Report of Session 2007–2008).

82 Ibid.

83 Roman Tomasic, "The Rescue of Northern Rock: Nationalization in the Shadow of Insolvency" (2009), <https://www.researchgate.net/publication/228298949_The_Rescue_of_Northern_Rock_Nationalization_in_the_Shadow_of_Insolvency>, Accessed: May 05, 2018.

84 HC Deb, January 26, 2008, Vol. 1. (House of Commons Treasury Committee, The Run on the Rocks, fifth Report of Session 2007–2008).

85 Patrik J. McConnell, "Northern Rock – The Group That Thinks Together, Sinks Together" (December 20, 2012), <https://papers.ssrn.com/sol3/papers.cfm?abstract_id=2204132>, Accessed: May 05, 2018.

should provide liquidity assistance to all financial institutions which are facing troubles, but its assistance should be conditional; otherwise, the frequency in the operations of LOLR can ignite a bigger disaster. The CB should demand collateral from the institutions before imparting liquidity, and the value of the collaterals must be able to fulfil the cost of liquidity support offered by the CB. The liquidity support should only be for illiquid but solvent financial institutions. Nonetheless, appraisal of the previous financial crises enunciates that it is hard to recognise whether the financial institution is merely illiquid or if it is facing the problems of solvency.[86]

Additionally, it was suggested that CBs must make their LOLR policy clear before the crisis and charge a high penalty rate on the support of liquidity.[87] The acumen behind these suggestions was to minimise the moral hazard problems. However, if a financial institution is large enough that its failure can cause a financial crisis, but the institution is unable to comprehend the policies imposed by the CB on the support of LOLR, the CB will still be compelled to rescue those institutions because it is the responsibility of the CB to protect the system. In such a situation, all the principles to curtail the effects of moral hazard problems seemed unhandy. Notwithstanding, the BOE used a new approach in the case of Northern Rock and nationalised it by using the powers it was granted in the Banking Act, 2008. The Act was enacted in special circumstances that empower the CB to take all appropriate measures which are necessary to maintain stability in the financial system.[88]

Nationalisation is also a proposed method to minimise the effects of moral hazard problems in a case when the LOLR has no other option but to rescue a financial institution. The Northern Rock Bank has started facing a major liquidity crisis in September 2007. Initially, the bank tried to handle the situation by converting its illiquid assets into liquid, but eventually, it reached a situation where the only option left for its survival was the intervention of the BOE as the LOLR. The evaluation of the situation of the concerned bank revealed that the bank is badly administered and heavily involved in risky activities without bothering about the repercussions. In the past, the BOE has used its discretionary powers and refused to play the role of LOLR for many financial institutions that were not meeting the standards of obtaining such support.[89] However, the case of Northern Rock was special because the directors of the BOE, after thoroughly examining its impact on the system,

86 Hyun Song, "Reflections on Northern Rock: The Bank Run That Heralded the Global Financial Crisis", <https://www.bis.org/publ/shin_2009.pdf>, Accessed: May 05, 2018.

87 See Chapter two (Walter Baghot).

88 Andrew Hauser, "LOLR Operations during the Financial Crisis: Seven Practical Lessons from the United Kingdom" (October 08, 2014) BIS Paper No. 79e, Accessed: November 14, 2018.

89 Roman Tomasic, "The Rescue of Northern Rock: Nationalization in the Shadow of Insolvency" (2009), <https://www.researchgate.net/publication/228298949_The_Rescue_of_Northern_Rock_Nationalization_in_the_Shadow_of_Insolvency>, Accessed: May 05, 2018.

concluded that its failure will badly affect the entire system. A whopping amount of £28 billion was injected to rescue the concerned bank. However, the bank was nationalised in the process of rescue. The BOE has used the same approach for nonbank financial institutions and nationalised them – e.g., Rolls Royce (1971) and British Leyland Ltd (1975). There are many cases in which the BOE has refused to play the role of LOLR for many financial institutions, which are illustrated in the chapter of critical evaluation of this research.[90]

The role of the Federal Reserve as the LOLR contributed a lot in handling the damages of the financial crises of different eras. The banking system of the US faced more financial crises than any other developed country. It was argued by economists that the banking system of the US was running without a CB, which made it more vulnerable because it is examined that trivial liquidity issues resulted in the collapse of the banks that could be addressed by injecting liquidity. The banks were lending liquidity to each other during financial troubles, but the absence of an official LOLR let the financial dreads spread among the investors. Consequently, many banks collapsed.[91] The inception of FRB has strengthened the financial system of the US, and the frequent failure of banks was stopped. The FRA is also empowered to lend liquidity to financial institutions which can provide collateral. A financial institution, no matter how big, can be denied liquidity assistance by the CB if it fails to meet the required criteria for obtaining the support of LOLR. Although it is the responsibility of each CB to protect the system against the financial crisis, if the CB has an opinion that the institutions which are demanding liquidity support are insolvent and liquidity support will not protect it from collapsing, it can use its discretionary powers and abstain from acting as LOLR.[92]

Lehman Brothers, a banking company, was established in 1850, and it continued to operate successfully before September 2007. It was regarded as one of the largest banking companies in the US; hence, it had a deep impact on the system. The concerned company started facing financial troubles in 2007, and like all other financial institutions, it had tried to overcome the issue. However, the administration of Lehman Brothers had reached a stage where the company can only be protected from collapsing by the intervention of FRB as LOLR. The case played a significant role in the progression of LOLR not only in the US but around the globe. The main criticism of the role of LOLR was that it is nothing but a rescue package for those financial institutions which

90 Dalvinder Singh, "U.K. Approach to Financial Crisis Management" (2010) *Transnational Law & Contemporary Problems*, Vol. 19, Page No. 872–927.

91 Jon R. Moen and Ellis W. Tallman, "Why Didn't the United States Establish a CB until after the Panic of 1907?" (January 25, 2015) FBR Atlanta Working Paper Series No. 1999–16, Accessed: November 12, 2018.

92 John A. Weinberg, "The Pursuit of Financial Stability: Essays from the Federal Reserve Bank of Richmond Annual Reports" (2015) *Economic Quarterly*, No. 1Q, Page No. 1–4.

are badly governed. It was evinced, in this case, that the support of LOLR is not for particular financial institutions but the entire system. In the banking history of the US, the bankruptcy of Lehman Brothers is regarded as the biggest one.[93]

This case has established that merely lending liquidity to the financial institutions which are facing the shortage of it is not the entire role of LOLR, but it can protect the system by taking more appropriate steps. Furthermore, it has also demonstrated that it is not necessary for the CBs to impart liquidity to the large institutions, even if they are unable to meet the standardised criteria. The demand for liquidity by investors urged the concerned company to seek assistance from the FRB. However, after a deliberate perusal of the case of Lehman Brothers, the FBR decided to use its discretionary powers and refused to rescue it. Although it was understandable that, if the FBR will refuse to rescue the concerned company, it will collapse and leave adverse effects on the system, the FRB decided not to intervene as LOLR.[94]

The directors of the FBR argued that administrative flaws of the Lehman Brothers influenced their decisions to refuse the liquidity support to it.[95] Deceptive matters were used to conceal the actual situation of the company from the stakeholders. Dodgy financial statements were made to show that the company is earning money by using the Repo 105 Procedure.[96] Shareholders of a company play the role of surveillant and make the directors accountable for their misdeeds. However, the directors of the concerned company had established an equivocal system so that shareholders cannot understand the business activities of the company. Investing in sub-prime mortgages turned out to be a major cause of the failure of many banking companies in the US during the financial crisis of 2007–2008. Lehman Brothers had also invested in sub-prime mortgages, even after being cautioned by the FRB.[97]

The FBR was criticised for its decision to abstain from playing the role of LOLR for Lehman Brothers, but its decision made it vehemently clear that the support of LOLR is not for financial institutions, no matter how large they are,

93 John M. Kawaku Mansha, "The Failure of Lehman Brothers: Causes, Preventive Measures and Recommendations" (March 02, 2015), <https://papers.ssrn.com/sol3/papers.cfm?abstract_id=2156006>, Accessed: November 08, 2018.

94 Kwabena Boamah, "The Collapse of Lehman Brothers: How It Happened?" (August 15, 2011), <https://www.researchgate.net/publication/228132583_The_Collapse_of_Lehman_Brothers_-_How_it_Happened>, Accessed: November 08, 2018.

95 John M. Kawaku Mansha, "The Failure of Lehman Brothers: Causes, Preventive Measures and Recommendations" (March 02, 2015), <https://papers.ssrn.com/sol3/papers.cfm?abstract_id=2156006>, Accessed: November 08, 2018.

96 An accounting trick in which a company classifies a short-term loan as a sale and subsequently uses the cash proceeds from said sale to reduce its liabilities.

97 Dimitios V. Sisko, "Lehman Brothers Case: Failure, Prevention and Recommendations" (November 22, 2013), <https://www.thinkingfinance.info/uploads/1/7/7/1/17713111/dimitrios_siskos.pdf>, Accessed: November 10, 2018.

who are unable to meet the regulatory requirements. The acumen behind this decision was to curtail more hazard problems and sent a resounding message to the administrators of the financial institutions that they will only be rescued if they will be able to satisfy that they were not involved in risky activities without considering the repercussions. Although it was a failure of a large financial institution that was influential in the system, it left several lessons for the CBs around the world which are facing criticism because of the moral hazard problems.[98]

On the other hand, the FRB has played the role of LOLR for American International Group (AIG), which is also an important example because of its comparison with the case of Lehman Brothers. AIG is not only one of the largest companies in the US, but it is also ranked among one of the largest companies in the world which are operating in more than 130 countries.[99] The main business of this company was to provide insurance to financial institutions, and several banks were also insured by it. This company was playing the role of LOLR for the financial institutions which were its customers. The company provided funds to the institutions which faced financial troubles. However, it was governing its business on certain rules and only offered its insurance to the institutions which were adhering to its rules. The financial crisis of 2007–2008 damaged many financial institutions around the world. Hence, many banks and financial institutions which were insured by AIG started facing a liquidity crisis and started claiming their insurance from the company.[100]

A frequency in the failure of banks and financial institutions which were insured by AIG has created liquidity shortfall for the company. Panic among the investors due to the financial crisis has made the situation worse and made a situation for the company in which it was unable to fulfil the demand of liquidity, even after a swift sale of its illiquid assets. After utilising all the possible resources and effectors, the management of the AIG decided to seek assistance from the FRB to play the role of LOLR and impart liquidity. This case was not directly handled merely by the FBR but due to the emergency created by the financial crisis; it was presented before the Senate, which, after a deliberate appraisal of the facts of the case, opted to rescue it. However, it was not merely rescued because it was too large and had a deep impact on the system. The facts of this case were different from the case of Lehman Brothers.[101]

98 Michael J. Fleming and Asani Sarkar, "The Failure Resolution of Lehman Brothers" *Economic Policy Review* (Forthcoming, April 10, 2014), Accessed: November 10, 2018.

99 Robert L. McDonald and Anna L. Paulson, "AIG in Hindsight" (April 2005), <https://www.nber.org/papers/w21108>, Accessed: November 09, 2018.

100 Anelize Slomp Aguiar, "The Controversies over the AIG's Collapse" (July 01, 2009), <https://papers.ssrn.com/sol3/papers.cfm?abstract_id=1435710>, Accessed: November 10, 2018

101 A. V. Narshimha Rao, "AIG Crisis: Impact on Insurance Business with Special Reference to China, Japan and India" (May 17, 2012), <https://papers.ssrn.com/sol3/papers.cfm?abstract_id=2061607>, Accessed: November 10, 2018.

AIG was not involved in risky activities, nor was it managed by a corrupt administration. The company was not using any techniques to avoid the implementation of regulations. The company was running its business without bothering about the repercussions just because of the confidence of having the FBR at their back as LOLR. This example is very important in the history of bailouts by CBs, which has left several lessons for financial institutions. In the modern business environment, the liquidity crisis can be ignited due to many reasons and cause a situation for a financial institution in which the institution requires liquidity support from the LOLR.[102] Thus, the intervention of LOLR varies from case to case, as illustrated previously in this part of the research. In many cases, liquidity support was denied on the grounds that the financial institution which was seeking the assistance could not provide collateral. On the other hand, many institutions were rescued even without demanding the collateral. Therefore, after the recent financial crisis, the US has regulated the role of LOLR by enacting the Dodd-Frank Act, 2010. However, in the UK, the BOE still possesses several discretionary powers while acting as LOLR.[103]

## 5.6 Lessons from the System of UK and US for Pakistan

The role of the banking system and financial institutions in the growth of a national income cannot be denied because, after the inception of the banking system, the growth has become much faster than it ever was before. However, the banking system has its weaknesses, as well, which can be detrimental for the economic system, especially in an environment of financial panic. Dread among the depositors is the most hazardous thing for the financial system because it drastically increases the demand for liquidity and leaves no window for the financial system to survive without seeking liquidity assistance from other institutions that can provide liquidity.[104] CBs are inevitable to implement the financial policies of the State and regulate the banking and other financial institutions. Additionally, ensuring the trust of the investor and help the financial institutions by injecting liquidity in times of financial emergencies is also an integral part of the duties of CBs.[105]

102 Robert L. McDonald and Anna L. Paulson, "AIG in Hindsight" (April 2005), <https://www.nber.org/papers/w21108>, Accessed: November 09, 2018.

103 Matthew Schoenfeld, "Aligning Incentives: How to Make Dodd-Frank Work" (May 10, 2012), <https://papers.ssrn.com/sol3/papers.cfm?abstract_id=2055893>, Accessed: November 11, 2018.

104 Dietrich Domanski, Richhild Moessner, and William R. Nelson, "CBs as LOLR: Experiences during the 2007–2010 Crisis and Lessons for the Future" (January 11, 2015) FEDS Working Paper No. 2014-110, Accessed: November 13, 2018.

105 Gillian Tett, "Have We Learnt the Lessons of the Financial Crisis?", *Financial Times* (August 31, 2018), Accessed: November 13, 2018.

The SBP is established on the model of the BOE and is empowered to protect the financial institutions by lending liquidity against a crisis. The banking system of Pakistan is emerging and can learn from the experiences of the BOE and FRB because they have played an important role to strengthen the financial system of the UK and the US during their respective crises. It was recognised by the policymakers of the UK in nineteenth century that the collapse of the financial institutions could be prevented if the BOE intervened and lent liquidity.[106] Furthermore, the issue of moral hazard problems has turned out to be the main hindrance to the evolution of the role of LOLR. Henry Thornton (1802) and Walter Bagehot (1873) suggested the framework for the operations of LOLR. In the UK, it was observed that the BOE possessed several discretionary powers as the LOLR, as was discussed previously in the example of Northern Rock.[107]

The BOE used the basic principles of LOLR in several cases and refused to rescue the banks and many financial institutions which were unable to provide good collateral. Notwithstanding, it can also be realised that, where it became essential to protect a financial institution the failure of which could harm the entire system, the BOE has superseded the rules and rescued financial institutions without bothering about the availability of collateral. A frequent dependency on financial institutions and their inability to produce collateral can also harm the system even more severely. Thus, to curtail the effects of moral hazard problems in the case of Northern Rock Bank, the BOE has realised that the failure of the concerned bank can contribute a lot to the effects of the financial crisis; that is why the BOE opted to rescue it and imparted liquidity.[108] However, the concerned bank was heavily involved in risky activities and could not provide collateral. Therefore, instead of leaving the money provided by the BOE in the administration of the bank, they decided to nationalise it. In the UK, the LOLR is authorised to take all appropriate steps which are necessary to deter financial crisis. There are no hard and fast rules imposed on the powers of BOE while playing the role of LOLR. To establish an invulnerable economic system, the government of the UK has enacted regulations to make the banking and financial system transparent.[109]

Moreover, the role of the FRB as a LOLR in financial crises also provides insights into the establishment of an economic system that addresses the challenges of modern financial and banking institutions. Before the establishment of

106 Michael Anson, David Bholat, Miao Kang, and Ryland Thomas, "The Bank of England as LOLR: New Historical Evidence from Daily Transaction Date" (November 17, 2017) Bank of England Working Paper No. 691, Accessed: March 03, 2018.

107 Andrew Hauser, "LOLR Operations during the Financial Crisis: Seven Practical Lessons from the United Kingdom" (October 08, 2014) BIS Paper No. 79e, Accessed: November 14, 2018.

108 Chris Giles, "Bank of England Defends Response to Financial Crisis after Criticism", *Financial Times Economics Editor* (April 10, 2018), Accessed: November 13, 2018.

109 Andrew Hauser, "LOLR Operations during the Financial Crisis: Seven Practical Lessons from the United Kingdom" (October 08, 2014) BIS Paper No. 79e, Accessed: November 14, 2018.

FBR, the system of the US was governed without having a CB for a long time, but eventually, the policymakers concluded that a CB is inevitable for a banking system to maintain stability against financial panics. The FBR's powers to act as LOLR was strictly based on the principles that it could only lend liquidity to the banks which can provide good collateral. However, after the Great Depression, the powers of the FBR were revisited and enhanced through an amendment in the Federal Reserve Act, 1913. It was then allowed to rescue the nonbanking institutions as well, and restrictions regarding collateral were also loosened. The powers of FBR as a LOLR were again amended after the recent financial crisis of 2007–2008 by the enactment of the Dodd-Frank Act, 2010.[110]

In Pakistan, the SBP plays the role of LOLR for its financial institutions, which is empowered by the State Bank of Pakistan Act, 1956. The SBP can only impart liquidity to the financial institutions which provide worthy collateral. The laws relating to the powers of the SBP as LOLR are explained in Chapter 4 of this research. The financial institutions of Pakistan were rescued by its CB many times; however, a frequent engagement in playing the role of LOLR caused stability issues for the SBP. Therefore, the IMF was asked to play the role of LOLR for the SBP.[111] Pakistan must bring transparency to its banking and financial institutions and stop imparting liquidity to the public financial institutions which are not returning it and surging financial pressure on the CB. Pakistan can learn from the example of Northern Rock Bank, in which the BOE could not let it collapse, but at the same time, was reluctant to provide liquidity to the same administration. Therefore, they decided to nationalise it and save the institution and the money which was used in rescuing it. Pakistan must also learn from the system of the US and implement the laws like Dodd-Frank Act, which can regulate the powers of the CB while acting as LOLR. The LOLR for Islamic banking in Pakistan is also not decided yet, which needs to be addressed immediately.[112] The approach of SBP was not befitting, as mentioned in the foregoing case study. Additionally, the evaluation of the examples of the UK and USA provides many lessons to inform regulatory reforms in Pakistan.

## 5.7 Functions of the Lender of Last Resort

In the modern economic system, it is a common fact that financial institutions can face liquidity shortages, and it is only the CB of the State which is empowered to generate liquidity to fulfil its demand. There is no separate institution

110 William R. Nelson, "Lessons from LOLR Actions during the Crisis: The Federal Reserve Experience" (October 08, 2014) BIS Paper No. 79d, Accessed: November 14, 2018.

111 Sara Cheema, "The IMF: Pakistan's History and Future with The LOLR", *Eurasia Review News & Analysis* (June 19, 2017), Accessed: November 13, 2018.

112 Asad Sayeed and Zubair Faisal Abbasi, "The Role of CBs in Supporting Economic Growth and Creation of Productive Employment: The Case of Pakistan" (2015) Employment Policy Department, Employment Working Paper No. 171, Accessed: November 14, 2018

that is authorised to exercise the powers of LOLR. It is a vigorous part of the duties of CBs at the domestic level, and the IMF, which is a branch of the World Bank, performs the duties of LOLR at the international level.[113] Usually, the understanding of LOLR is that the CBs intervene by lending liquidity to financial institutions which are in need of liquidity. The uncertain situation of the financial system and surging panic among investors invoke the operations of LOLR to enhance the resistance of the financial institutions against a crisis.[114] However, the impartation of liquidity by private individuals or institutions to financial markets cannot attribute the role of LOLR to them because it is a part but not the entire function of this role. This role is not limited only to providing liquidity but has several functions. The stability of the financial system lies in the trust of the depositors; however, ups and downs are part of its activities.[115] In modern financial systems, institutions are working with each other; hence, they provide loans to financial institutions which are facing problems. However, in some circumstances, when they are unable to handle the issue and CB realises that it could be detrimental for the system, it operates as a LOLR.[116]

In 1797, Sir Francis Baring argued that the BOE holds this power to lend liquidity when all other financial institutions failed to do so. Henry Thornton and Walter Bagehot have designed the characteristics of LOLR and explained the insight behind its operations.[117] The impartation of liquidity in the apprehension of a financial crisis is different from lending a loan. The CBs have the responsibility to govern the system, not to protect individual institutions. Therefore, liquidity assistance in the operations of LOLR can only be granted to solvent institutions.[118] The core function of the CBs as a LOLR is not to intervene during special circumstances, but it is obligated to take all necessary steps to make an indomitable system. The dread of a crisis is more annihilating for the survival of the system than the shortage of liquidity. It is a vital part of the functions of the LOLR to ensure the trust of the stakeholder in the system.[119] The reason behind establishing a CB is to have an institution that

113 Henery C. Wallich, “Central Banks as Regulators and Lenders of Last Resort in an International Context: A View from the United States”, <https://link.springer.com/chapter/10.1007/978-1-349-07927-8_13>, Accessed: March 13, 2018.

114 Curzio Giannini, “The IMF and LOLR Function: An External View” (1999) *Finance & Development*, Vol. 36, No. 3, Page No. 1.

115 Stanley Fischer, “The Lender of Last Resort Function in the United States” (2016) *International Finance*, Vol. 2, Page No. 239–60.

116 Thomas M. Humphrey, “LOLR: The Concept in History” (1989) *FRB Richmond Economic Review*, Vol. 75, No. 2, Page No. 8.

117 Robert E. Keleher and Thomas M. Humphery, “The Lender of Last Resort: A Historical Perspective” (1984) *Cato Journal*, Vol. 4, No. 1, Page No. 275.

118 Stanley Fischer, “The Lender of Last Resort Function in the United States” (2016) *International Finance*, Vol. 2, Page No. 239–60.

119 Michael D. Bordo, “Rules for a Lender of Last Resort: An Historical Perspective” (2014) *Journal of Economic Dynamics and Control*, Vol. 49, Page No. 126.

can regulate the financial system and also have the power to implement its policies.[120]

The functions of LOLR are enhanced, and it is no more a mere facility to provide liquidity during a crisis; it is regarded as a tool to govern the economic system. Thus, monitoring the financial policy of the State is also an important part of this role.[121] It must have an accurate check and balance on the system and identify insolvent financial institutions. The regulations regarding the functions of LOLR must make clear in which circumstances and on which grounds its assistance can be availed. It also ensures the trust of the domestic and foreign investors in the system by taking all necessary steps.[122] According to the needs of the system, it provides opportunities for the financial systems to excel in their businesses. Finally, if the financial institutions start facing liquidity shortages and are unable to overcome their problem by the normal loan facilities of the market,[123] the CB extends its support of liquidity as a LOLR to abolish the problem of liquidity and curtail the panic of a crisis. The mandate of the role of LOLR is not limited to impart liquidity, but it can also purchase the illiquid assets of the financial institutions which are in trouble.[124] Normally, to fulfil the demand for liquidity, financial institutions start selling their illiquid assets, and a rapid sale always deteriorates the value of the assets and makes the situation worse for the institutions to handle. Therefore, the functions of LOLR are not limited to certain operations; it can go to any limit for the survival of the system.[125]

The functions of an international LOLR are limited, as compared to those of the domestic one. It is no more a contention whether the modern global economic system requires an international LOLR or not. The failure of the domestic system has effacing effects on the world's economy.[126] Financial institutions seek help from CBs when they face difficulties, and the CBs, in their difficult times, ask the IMF, which is currently working as an ILOLR, to rescue them.[127] It can ask foreign investors to invest in the country which is facing liquidity problems or ensure the existing investors that it will rescue

120 Gerald P. O'Driscoll, Jr., "Why Do We Have a CB?", *The Wall Street Journal*, Vol. 37, No. 2, Page No. 285–291 (December 03, 2010), Accessed: April 10, 2018.

121 Paul Tucker, "The LOLR and Modern Central Banking: Principles and Reconstruction" (2014) *Bank for International Settlement*, Page No. 10.

122 Kathryn Judge, "The Role of a Modern Lender of Last Resort" (2016) *Columbia Law Review*, Vol. 116, Page No. 843.

123 Paul Tucker, "The LOLR and Modern Central Banking: Principles and Reconstruction" (2014) *Bank for International Settlement*, Page No. 10.

124 Ibid.

125 Maurice Obstfeld, "LOLR in Globalized World" (November 2009), Accessed: March 02, 2018.

126 Edwin M. Truman, "The IMF as an International Lender of Last Resort" (Peterson Institute for International Economics, October 12, 2010), Accessed: February 04, 2018.

127 Jean-Pierre Landau, "International LOLR: Some Thoughts for 21st Century" (2014) *Bank for International Settlement*, No. 79, Page No. 119.

the CB if needed, which eliminates the panic and allows the system to stabilise itself.[128] The ILOLR can play the role of a consultant; however, it cannot determine the financial policy of the State. Like the domestic LOLR, the IMF cannot purchase the assets of the CB which requires its assistance. It can make its support conditional that the CB which needs its help must provide a viable financial policy that will be able to return the money.[129]

In the modern economic era, the significance of LOLR cannot be denied. Its salient functions and successful role in the recent financial crisis make it an inseparable part of the functions of the CBs at the domestic and IMF at the international level.[130] Liquidity shortage and minor financial panics are common in the current financial systems and can be converted into a large financial crisis in the absence of an institution that can lend liquidity to address such problems.[131] A trivial liquidity issue can escalate the apprehensions of crisis and make it difficult for even a solvent institution to survive. Large financial institutions, in the absence of a LOLR, will be mighty in the financial system and will make the conditions of loan facilities unapproachable for small institutions.[132] The rationale behind having a LOLR on a domestic and international level is not merely to have an institution that will provide liquidity in difficult times but to make such an effective and efficient system where all institutions enjoy the same rights and can excel. However, to achieve this goal, proper legislation is required to regulate this role according to the insights of having it.[133]

## 5.8 Federal Reserves, Bank of England and State Bank of Pak as LOLR

### *5.8.1 Federal Reserves as LOLR*

Every financial system requires a CB to maintain the stability of the system and back the financial institutions in tough economic conditions. The first CB for the United States was created in 1791, and it was known as the Bank of the United States. It was established to fulfil the traditional duties of a CB to assist the federal government in its financial matters. It was authorised to emit notes which were accepted by the federal government in making financial

128 Ibid.

129 Edwin M. Truman, "The IMF as an International Lender of Last Resort" (Peterson Institute for International Economics, October 12, 2010), Accessed: February 04, 2018.

130 Paul Tucker, "The LOLR and Modern Central Banking: Principles and Reconstruction" (2014) *Bank for International Settlement*, Page No. 10.

131 Ibid.

132 Jean-Pierre Landau, "International LOLR: Some Thoughts for 21st Century" (2014) *Bank for International Settlement*, No. 79, Page No. 119.

133 Maurice Obstfeld, "LOLR in Globalized World" (November 2009), Accessed: March 02, 2018.

payments.[134] Though it was not well accepted unanimously by the inhabitants of the USA, its private ownership allows it to work as an independent institution rather than as a government institution. Hence, even after 20 years, it was unable to get approval from Congress to continue working as a CB. In 1836, President Andrew Jackson used his powers and rejected the bill of the extension of the second CB of the US.[135] The absence of a CB was causing harm to the system and the country faced many financial crises in 1839, 1857, 1873, 1893 and 1907. It was realised that the presence of an institution which can give monetary policy and help the financial institutions when they face liquidity problems will curb the occurrence of these crises. Minor financial institutions can create panic among the creditors and create a situation where the financial institutions will be unable to address it. The CBs are designed to help the financial institutions when the demand for liquidity rises and prevent financial crisis. CBs were collaterals; hence, they were lending liquidity to solvent institutions and allowed them to fulfil the demand of liquidity without selling off their assets. At the outset of the twentieth century, the US did not have a CB; hence, it had faced many crises, one after another.[136] Finally, the financial crisis of 1907 paved the way for the establishment of Federal Reserve, though many economists were still opposing the idea of having a CB and were arguing that the powers should be granted to regional bodies.[137]

The Federal Reserve Act (FRA), 1913 empowered the Federal Reserve to play the role of LOLR and lend liquidity to financial institutions which were facing liquidity shortages. In the recent global crisis, the role of the Federal Reserve is commendable, as it took a radical approach to deter the crisis.[138] It did not rely on traditional lending policies and took an unconventional step to prevent financial institutions from collapsing, which also played an important role in extending the conception of LOLR. Sections 10-B, 13 and 14 of FRA, 1913 legalised the operations of the Federal Reserve as LOLR. At the starting of 2007, the Federal Reserve lent liquidity to the financial markets to enable them to resist crisis. Although Bagehot emphasised that a high-interest rate should be charged to curtail moral hazard problems, it was reduced to

134 Jerome H. Powell, "America's Central Bank: The History and Structure of the Federal Reserves" (2017), <https://www.bis.org/review/r170330d.pdf>, Accessed: April 20, 2018.

135 Ibid.

136 Gayane Oganesyan, "The Changed Role of LOLR: Crisis Responses of Federal Reserves, European CB and Bank of England" (2013) Institute for International Political Economy Berlin 19/2013, Accessed: March 30, 2018.

137 Jerome H. Powell, "America's Central Bank: The History and Structure of the Federal Reserves" (2017), <https://www.bis.org/review/r170330d.pdf>, Accessed: April 20, 2018. Ibid.

138 Hansjörg Herr, Sina Rüdiger, and Jennifer Pédussel Wu, "The Federal Reserve as LOLR During the Subprime Crisis – Successful Stabilisation Without Structural Changes" (2016) Working Paper No. 65/2016, Accessed: April 20, 2018.

encourage the banking sector to lend to each other, which worked well to stabilise the system.[139] The Federal Reserve completely ignored the principles of Bagehot and directly lent to the insolvent institutions. It lent freely to the AIG company, which worked well to stabilise it.[140] The Federal Reserve also followed the examples of the Bank of England and purchased the illiquid assets of the financial institutions which were forced to sell them rapidly because of the liquidity demand. This step provided liquidity to the financial institutions and also prevented the depreciation of their assets.[141]

The role of LOLR is regarded as a vital part of the modern economic system; however, it was not warmly accepted by many economists because of the moral hazard problems. In the case of Lehman Brothers when the Federal Reserve refused to lend liquidity, it was badly criticised by economists. It was perhaps the biggest bankruptcy in the history of the United States and left many lessons for the financial institution to be learned.[142] The presence of LOLR allows financial institutions to ignore the consequences of risky investment because they believe that they will eventually be rescued if there will be a panic, which creates moral hazard problems. It is extensively described in the part on moral hazard in this research.[143] To address the issue of moral hazard problems, the Federal Reserve has set an apt precedent in the case of the Lehman Brothers. Although, the Federal Reserve has played a very effective role in resisting financial crisis, even then, it was observed that there are many gaps in the legislation, and this significant role cannot be left at the discretion of the Federal Reserve; therefore, it needs to be legislated.[144] The United States, which was struggling to have a CB which can play a role of LOLR when the financial institutions need liquidity, is now leading in expanding the doctrine of LOLR. After the failure of the recent financial crisis to address the loopholes of the existing laws and fix the moral hazard problems, the United States has enforced the Dodd-Frank Act, 2010. It provides principles on which the financial institutions will be provided with liquidity.[145]

139 Gayane Oganesyan, "The Changed Role of LOLR: Crisis Responses of Federal Reserves, European CB and Bank of England" (2013) Institute for International Political Economy Berlin 19/2013, Accessed: March 30, 2018.

140 Ibid, Page No. 12.

141 Marc Dobler, Simon Gray, Diarmuid Murphy, and Bozena Radzewicz-Bak, "The LOLR Function after the Global Financial Crisis" (2016) IMF Working Paper No. 16/10, ISBN: 9781498355995/1018-5941, Assessed: May 17, 2017.

142 Kwabena Boamah, "The Collapse of Lehman Brothers – How It Happened?" (August 15, 2011), <https://www.researchgate.net/publication/228132583_The_Collapse_of_Lehman_Brothers_-_How_it_Happened>, Accessed: March 09, 2018.

143 See the part of Moral Hazard Problems.

144 Paul Tucker, "The LOLR and Modern Central Banking: Principles and Reconstruction" (2014) *Bank for International Settlement*, Page No. 10.

145 Kathryn Judge, "The Role of a Modern Lender of Last Resort" (2016) *Columbia Law Review*, Vol. 116, Page No. 843.

### *5.8.2 Bank of England as LOLR*

This part of the research explains how the Bank of England (BOE) adhered to the insights of Sir Francis Baring and played the role of LOLR for the financial institutions during the crisis. It is important to appraise the operations of LOLR in previous crises to get guidance. As Lord Mervyn King said, "During the crisis, I found that the study of earlier periods was more illuminating than any amount of econometric modelling".[146] The evolution of the LOLR is extensively described in Chapter 1.1 – that, although the BOE had lent liquidity, in the eighteenth-century, to the financial institutions when they need it, it is a duty of the CB, which was established in the last quarter of the nineteenth century.[147] It is important to evaluate if the BOE has altered its policies after accepting the role of LOLR or not. There is no evidence that can enunciate that there was an empirical change in the policies of BOE henceforth. It was criticised for its primary aims of profit maximisation and the presence of a conflict of interest, and therefore, it could not hold the position of CB.[148]

The BOE has played the role of LOLR in the crisis of 1847, 1857 and 1866. Bagehot, in his book *Lombard Street* (1873), described the rules for LOLR which were followed by CBs around the world.[149] Bagehot's doctrine has three main principles of lending: i) the CB must lend freely, ii) it must lend at a high-interest rate, iii) its lending must be against worthy collateral. Although it can be evinced by the operations of the BOE as LOLR that it has freely lent liquidity, it was lent only to few institutions.[150] Like the other CBs, there were no regulations regarding LOLR. Thus, BOE has also used its discretionary powers and lent three-fourths of the total amount of liquidity to the top five borrowers.[151] The principle of charging a high-interest rate was strictly followed in the crises of 1857 and 1866. The interest rate was more than the commonly practised rate. Nonetheless, in the crisis of 1847, the interest rate on the lending of BOE was even below the normal market rates. Therefore, it can be argued that there was no absolute condition for the lending of liquidity in the operations of LOLR because the CBs lent liquidity on lower interest rates to strengthen the system.[152] Finally, the principle of

146 Lord Mervyn King former governor of the Bank of England.

147 Esther Madeleine Ogden, "The Development of the Role of the Bank of England as a LOLR, 1870–1914" (September 1988), <https://www.semanticscholar.org/paper/The-development-of-the-role-of-the-Bank-of-England-Ogden/fc021a08a20210f2e7f958d8b655c29eb9c7dc87>, Accessed: April 26, 2018.

148 See Chapter 1.1.

149 Mike Anson, David Bholat, Miao Kang, and Ryland Thomas, "The Bank of England as LOLR: New Historical Evidence from Daily Transactional Data" (November 2007) Staff Working Paper No. 691, Accessed: March 03, 2018.

150 Ibid.

151 Ibid, Page No. 3.

152 Gayane Oganesyan, "The Changed Role of LOLR: Crisis Responses of Federal Reserves, European CB and Bank of England" (2013) Institute for International Political Economy Berlin 19/2013, Accessed: March 30, 2018.

lending against worthy collateral was also practised, but the BOE has again used its discretionary powers to evaluate the collaterals and did not follow the same rules for all enterprises.[153]

The principle behind the operations of LOLR is that it will only intervene and lend liquidity to the financial institutions which are experiencing liquidity problems but are not insolvent.[154] In the cases of Barings and Yorkshire Penny Bank (YPB), when both of them were unable to fulfil the demand for liquidity, assistance was sought from the BOE and they were rescued because they were illiquid and not insolvent.[155] However, in 1878, the City of Glasgow Bank (CGB) was refused liquidity support because the collaterals which were produced by the CGB were not accepted as good securities. It is, however, an unaddressed issue how a CB can determine if the financial institution is illiquid or insolvent.[156] Baring was rescued and had established an argument that it was merely illiquid, but it took four years to settle its liabilities. Many institutions that were declared insolvent and could not get the support of LOLR would have been able to settle their liabilities had they been granted several years like other institutions. In the case of Northern Rock, the BOE has used an entirely different approach, and instead of lending liquidity, the BOE decided to nationalise it because it was not befitting for the system to let it fall on the grounds of not having good securities.[157]

Sir Paul Tucker[158] (2014) expressed his views that it was a tragedy that the role of LOLR was neglected in the major policy debates of central banking, and no effects have been made to legislate on it. Albeit, the significance of the LOLR in the modern financial system cannot be denied, but leaving its functions at the discretion of CB will be fatal.[159] The role of BOE as a LOLR during the financial crisis was well regarded by many economists; however, it is also emphasised by all the policy-makers that like the issue of moral hazard

153 Mike Anson, David Bholat, Miao Kang, and Ryland Thomas, "The Bank of England as LOLR: New Historical Evidence from Daily Transactional Data" (November 2007), Staff Working Paper No. 691, Accessed: March 03, 2018.

154 Esther Madeleine Ogden, "The Development of the Role of the Bank of England as a LOLR, 1870–1914" (September 1988), <https://www.semanticscholar.org/paper/The-development-of-the-role-of-the-Bank-of-England-Ogden/fc021a08a20210f2e7f958d8b655c29eb9c7de87>, Accessed: April 26, 2018.

155 Ibid.

156 Mike Anson, David Bholat, Miao Kang, and Ryland Thomas, "The Bank of England as LOLR: New Historical Evidence from Daily Transactional Data" (November 2007) Staff Working Paper No. 691, Accessed: March 03, 2018.

157 Roman Tomasic, "The Rescue of Northern Rock: Nationalization in the Shadow of Insolvency" (2009), <https://www.researchgate.net/publication/228298949_The_Rescue_of_Northern_Rock_Nationalization_in_the_Shadow_of_Insolvency>, Accessed: April 15, 2018.

158 Former Deputy Governor of the Bank of England.

159 Mike Anson, David Bholat, Miao Kang, and Ryland Thomas, "The Bank of England as LOLR: New Historical Evidence from Daily Transactional Data" (November 2007) Staff Working Paper No. 691, Accessed: March 03, 2018.

problem it is also important to frame a regulatory framework for the functions of LOLR. The absence of effective regulations will continue to allow the BOE to use its discretionary powers to judge if the financial institution is insolvent or merely illiquid. Hence, this role will remain controversial and it will not be possible to achieve the desired goals.[160]

### *5.8.3 State Bank of Pakistan as LOLR*

Pakistan is among the developing countries, and its banking sector is still evolving. State Bank of Pakistan (SBP) holds the gold resources of the country and has the power to emit notes. It is the only institution that can lend liquidity to financial institutions when no other institution is capable of lending.[161] The SBP plays the role of LOLR to strengthen the financial institutions against a crisis. However, its functions as being a LOLR are equivocal and still emerging. The State Bank of Pakistan Act, 1956 legalised the LOLR operations of SBP. Due to unprogressive financial policies and unproficiency in the operations of LOLR, Pakistan has faced a severe financial crisis.[162] In this modern era, the role of LOLR is not merely to lend liquidity in a crisis; it has several functions to protect the system from recession, as was described earlier in Chapters. The panic among the creditors is the most annihilating factor for the financial system, which the CB should eliminate while performing the role of LOLR. The SBP lent liquidity to many financial institutions to stabilise the system and issued a large number of new notes to fulfil the demand. However, the emittance of new notes rapidly deteriorated the value of the currency and caused inflation.[163] Therefore, Pakistan sought assistance from the IMF, which is playing the role of international LOLR.

The role of LOLR has emerged swiftly after the recent financial crisis in developed countries, especially in the UK and the USA. Nonetheless, it is still not part of major financial debates in the financial and economic forums of Pakistan.[164] Islamic banking is an emerging sector in Pakistan; however, there is no legislation and clear policy of the SBP as to who, in case this sector faces

160 Kathryn Judge, "The Role of a Modern Lender of Last Resort" (2016) *Columbia Law Review*, Vol. 116, Page No. 843.

161 Raja CRN, "Role and Functions of the State Bank of Pakistan" (August 22, 2009), Accessed: April 21, 2018.

162 Mateen Altaf, "Role of State Bank of Pakistan in Economic Development of the Country" (April 11, 2016), <https://words.pk/role-of-sbp-fbr-in-economic-development-of-pakistan/>, Accessed: April 21, 2018.

163 Muhammad Farooq Arby, "State Bank of Pakistan: Evolution, Functions and Organization" (March 2009) MPRA Paper No. 13614, Accessed: March 03, 2018.

164 Mateen Altaf, "Role of State Bank of Pakistan in Economic Development of the Country" (April 11, 2016), <<https://words.pk/role-of-sbp-fbr-in-economic-development-of-pakistan/>, Accessed: April 21, 2018.

a liquidity crisis, will play the role of LOLR.[165] There are no set principles for providing liquidity support, and it will not be befitting to adopt the principles of the UK or USA because each system has different needs and dimensions.[166] The banking sector is not the only one getting liquidity support from the SBP, but it also lends to government institutions like Pakistan International Airlines (PIA), Pakistan Steel Mill and Pakistan Railways, etc. Most financial and governmental institutions are unable to return the money to the SBP. The absence of strong regulations to curtail moral hazard problems is hauling the system towards crisis. Public money is going in vain, and due to moral hazard problems, the LOLR itself is becoming the cause of a recession. Thus, the SBP has had no other option but to seek assistance from the IMF.[167] Notwithstanding, it is a dilemma that Pakistan's economy is standing on the verge of destruction and miserably depending on the aid of IMF, but still, there are no financial regulations that can address these issues. Although the IMF is working as an ILOLR, it is alleged that it is influencing the economic systems of the countries, and its stipulations are fair for the developing countries.[168] This research aims to propose a regulatory framework for the functions of LOLR in Pakistan.

## 5.9 Criticism on the Role of LOLR

Imparting liquidity to financial institutions which are facing a shortage of liquidity and are unable to attain it by using their resources is a vital part of the role of LOLR.[169] In modern economic systems, CBs at the domestic and IMF at the international level are playing this role. Nonetheless, the conception of this role was nothing more than lending liquidity to financial institutions, or in some cases, to CBs. Therefore, this role was played by different companies, and even persons, and they lent liquidity, even in the nineteenth century.[170] The rationale behind this role is to prevent a financial institution from collapsing which can survive with the support of liquidity. In business activities, it is not astounding that even a solvent institution could face a deficiency of

165 Muhammad Umer, "LOLR for Islamic Banking under Review" (April 01, 2015), Accessed: April 23, 2018.

166 Muhammad Farooq Arby, "State Bank of Pakistan: Evolution, Functions and Organization" MPRA Paper No. 13614 (March 2009), Accessed: March 03, 2018.

167 Sara Cheema, "The IMF: Pakistan's History and Future with the LOLR", *Eurasia Review* (June 19, 2017), Accessed: April 21, 2018.

168 Edwin M. Truman, "The IMF as an International Lender of Last Resort" (Peterson Institute for International Economics, October 12, 2010), Accessed: February 04, 2018.

169 Paul Tucker, "The LOLR and Modern Central Banking: Principles and Reconstruction" (2014) *Bank for International Settlement*, Page No. 10.

170 Robert E. Keleher and Thomas M. Humphery, "The Lender of Last Resort: A Historical Perspective" (1984) *Cato Journal*, Vol. 4, No. 1, Page No. 275.

liquidity. A trivial liquidity issue can be converted into a severe financial crisis if there are no institutions that can lend liquidity in such circumstances.[171] The role of LOLR is one of the fundamental justifications for having a CB, and it has played an important role to control the financial crisis.[172]

Natural and legal persons are the owners of their assets; hence, if they are capable of offering liquidity support to other institutions working in the financial markets, then they are free to do so.[173] Liquidity support to the financial system in the domestic market or a CB can be based upon their personal or business benefits. Usually, private lenders lend liquidity to small business entities and earn profits by charging a high-interest rate.[174] In the operations of LOLR, private entities can gain or lose their money, which is their business activities; therefore, there is no point where policymakers can intrude. However, in a modern economic system, when the conception of LOLR is wider than merely lending liquidity, this role is officially played by the CBs.[175] The resources which the CBs hold are not owned by them because they possess all the resources and taxes of the State. It has more obligations towards the system than commercial banks or private financial institutions. The main justification behind the operations of LOLR conducted by the CBs is that the failure of some financial institutions can harm the entire system. Thus, its liquidity support is neither provided to the individual institutions nor is it unaccountable assistance.[176]

The collapse of a large financial institution can escalate the panic among domestic and international investors, which increases the demand for liquidity. Therefore, the policymakers argue that liquidity support helps such financial institutions to sustain themselves against the illiquidity crisis. The assurance of the CB to rescue financial institutions helps to curtail panic amongst creditors which is most annihilating for the survival of the system.[177] The responsibility of the CBs is to make a stabilised and prosperous economic system; hence, it is entirely in the favour of the public at large to play the role of LOLR. The operations of CBs as a LOLR are not like those of the private

171 Matthew C. Klein, "Do Lenders of Last Resort Actually Make the Financial System Safer?" (January 12, 2017), Accessed: December 10, 2017.

172 Ben O'Neill, "The LOLR: A Comparative Analysis of Central Banking and Fractional-Reserve Free Banking" (2013) *Libertarian Papers*, Vol. 5, No. 1, Page No. 163–86, Accessed: April 05, 2018.

173 Ibid.

174 Michael D. Bordo, "The LOLR: Alternative Views and Historical Experience", *Economic Review* (January/February 1990), Accessed: April 05, 2018.

175 Ulrich Bindseil and Luc Laeven, "Confusion about the LOLR" (January 13, 2017), Accessed: April 06, 2018.

176 Michael D. Bordo, "The LOLR: Alternative Views and Historical Experience", *Economic Review* (January/February 1990), Accessed: April 05, 2018.

177 Matthew C. Klein, "Do Lenders of Last Resort Actually Make the Financial System Safer?" (January 12, 2017), Accessed: December 10, 2017.

institutions; they must follow the rules set in the financial policies.[178] They lend liquidity to the institutions which can produce worthy collateral and are just illiquid, not insolvent. To fulfil the cost of such operations, a high-interest rate is being imposed.

Notwithstanding, there is a strong criticism of the CBs because of the role of LOLR. The financial institutions which have involvement in risky activities to earn high profits have no intention to share their profits with anyone apart from their shareholders.[179] However, the presence of LOLR assures that, if they will bear losses from risky activities, they will be rescued. The resources which are used in rescuing such financial institutions by the CBs belong to the nation. Hence, to use the money of the nation to fulfil the losses of a financial institution owned by a few individuals will mean extending the losses nationwide.[180] It is argued that the CBs are meant to announce the financial policy of the State and maintain the stability of the system. Although, in the apprehensions of the financial crisis, when the financial market is unable to provide sufficient liquidity support to the institutions facing troubles, the CB is the only institution that is empowered to issue new notes and control the situation. It is argued that the frequent issuing of new notes will deteriorate the value of the currency and cause inflation.[181]

The CBs were reluctant to play the role of LOLR and were opposing the presence of it because of its moral hazard problems. The evolution of economic systems has also led to the emergence of this role, and several proposals are suggested to curtail the issues of moral hazards.[182] LOLR has played a vital role to strengthen financial systems by CBs and IMF at domestic and international levels, respectively. Its operations during the crisis were, indeed, beneficial for the system; hence, its presence is considered inevitable in modern economic systems. However, CBs have used their discretionary powers to play this role because there was no proper legislation on it. Many insolvent financial institutions were rescued, and solvent institutions were refused liquidity support, which gives rise to several queries.[183] It was argued that financial institutions become illiquid because of mishandling, and the support

178 Marc Dobler, Simon Gray, Diarmuid Murphy, and Bozena Radzewicz-Bak, "The LOLR Function after the Global Financial Crisis" (2016) IMF Working Paper No. 16/10, ISBN: 9781498355995/1018-5941, Accessed: May 17, 2017.

179 Ben O'Neill, "The LOLR: A Comparative Analysis of Central Banking and Fractional-Reserve Free Banking" (2013) *Libertarian Papers*, Vol. 5, No. 1, Page No. 163–86, Accessed: April 05, 2018.

180 Dietrich Domanski, Richhild Moessner, and William Nelson, "CBs as LOLR: Experiences during the 2007–2010 Crisis and Lessons for the Future" (2014), Accessed: April 10, 2018.

181 Michael D. Bordo, "Rules for a Lender of Last Resort: An Historical Perspective" (2014) *Journal of Economic Dynamics and Control*, Vol. 49, Page No. 126.

182 Paul Tucker, "The LOLR and Modern Central Banking: Principles and Reconstruction" (2014) *Bank for International Settlement*, Page No. 10.

183 Matthew C. Klein, "Do Lenders of Last Resort Actually Make the Financial System Safer?" (January 12, 2017), Accessed: December 10, 2017.

of LOLR is a bonus for inefficient administrations.[184] Thus, the contemplations regarding the existence of LOLR cannot be neglected merely because a modern financial system will be unable to survive in the absence of LOLR. Though it is an established fact that its presence is needed, nonetheless, it cannot be left to the discretionary powers of the CBs. Proper legislation is as important as the existence of LOLR to make a less vulnerable economic system.[185]

## 5.10 Summary

This chapter has widely explained the powers of the BOE as a LOLR and argued on the laws which authorised it to act as a LOLR. The operations of the LOLR in the UK and the grounds on which liquidity support was offered have been discussed. The chapter has further explicated the factors behind the establishment of FBR and its role in curtailing financial anxiety from the economic system of the US. The powers of FRB to act as LOLR have been explored, and the key features of the Dodd-Frank Act, 2010 have been evaluated as well. The case of Northern Rock and the reasons for its nationalisation have been examined. The cases of Lehman Brothers and AIG have also been studied, as they played an imperative role in the progression of the role of LOLR. Finally, certain lessons for the system of Pakistan from the experiences of the UK and US have been derived by comparing the operational strategies of the BOE and FBR. This chapter has provided a critical evaluation of the role of LOLR. It has discussed the functions of LOLR and also explained that, if there will be no institution that will play the role of LOLR for the financial system in this modern system, the entire system can collapse because of a minor liquidity problem. LOLR can address the liquidity problem and eliminate pain among investors. This chapter has discussed the role of the Federal Reserve, the Bank of England and the State Bank of Pakistan as LOLR. It has also explained the laws of all three countries relating to the role of LOLR.

184 Ibid.

185 Dietrich Domanski, Richhild Moessner, and William Nelson, "CBs as LOLR: Experiences during the 2007–2010 Crisis and Lessons for the Future" (2014), Accessed: April 10, 2018.

# 6 Regulatory Reform Proposals and Conclusion

This chapter contains details about reforming the role of LOLR in Pakistan and explains how it would benefit the financial system of the country. All problems of the financial system of Pakistan which are discussed in the previous chapters and the lessons which are extracted after a deliberate examination of the systems of the UK and US regarding the role of LOLR are regarded as the key principles before proposing a way forward in this chapter. The first part describes the rules and regulations for the role of LOLR in the UK and US and unfolds the problems which were faced by the BOE and FRB in the past but were subsequently reformed at a later stage. The second part argues the limitations of the current legislation to address the financial problems in Pakistan and suggests reform proposals to make a modern system for LOLR. It concludes with a discussion on the implications of the suggested proposals.

## 6.1 System of LOLR in Pakistan

The State Bank of Pakistan is the CB in Pakistan which was established in 1948 and authorised to act as the LOLR for the financial institutions in its jurisdictions. Although the SBP was established on the model of BOE, the financial system of Pakistan has many similarities with the system of the US also. The financial system of Pakistan has gone through an intense process of evolution, and different models for the banking and financial institutions were employed. The financial system has progressed a lot, but it is still far from a developed system. The banking and financial system of Pakistan started with the investments of the private sector and aimed to attract foreign investment to establish a prosperous economic system. However, the unsatisfactory performance of the banking and financial sector urged policymakers to nationalise all the banking and financial institutions in the 1970s, which has been extensively discussed in Chapter 4 of this study. Additionally, the inability of this policy to deliver according to expectations and a paradigm shift of the political ideologies from the commercial system

DOI: 10.4324/9781003478768-6

to Islamisation again privatised the banking and other financial institutions in the 1990s.[1]

The inception of Islamic banking is another big change in the functioning of the banking sector in Pakistan. The SBP is authorised to lend liquidity to financial institutions which face liquidity challenges. However, unlike the BOE, the SBP is bound by the legislation to offer liquidity assistance to the financial institutions which can provide good collateral. In Pakistan, the government is the biggest borrower of the SBP to fulfil the demand of liquidity which urged the SBP to emit new notes without even holding the reserves at the back, and resultantly, it caused inflation. Many national institutions have been operating at a loss for a long time and the SBP is injecting liquidity into them for their survival. PIA, Pakistan Steel Mills and Pakistan Railways are the major examples that are continuously surviving on the liquidity support which the SBP is providing as a LOLR. It is clearly stated in section 17 of the State Bank of Pakistan Act, 1956 that the bank could provide liquidity support to financial institutions which could provide collateral, but the government is continuously superseding these rules by the ordinances which are coming every year and lending liquidity to these financial institutions.[2]

The role of LOLR was criticised for a long time after its inception due to the moral hazard problems, and it was argued by many economists that it would cause wastage of the national money. All theories relating to the role of LOLR indicate that, if a CB would be frequently engaged in the operations of LOLR, it would be annihilated for the entire system. It was warned that liquidity support must not be offered to financial institutions which were not capable of returning it. The BOE has denied its support as a LOLR to many financial institutions on the grounds that the financial institutions were not able to fulfill the requirements of the BOE that they would be able to return the money. In cases like Northern Rock Bank, when the BOE had no choice but to rescue it, the bank, instead of lending liquidity in the hands of the administration of the concerned bank, nationalised it because the acumen behind having a LOLR is to maintain stability in the financial system. Therefore, governments empowered their CBs with discretionary powers so that they can take all necessary steps to protect the system. The debacle of Lehman Brothers is still regarded as one of the biggest bankruptcies in the banking history of the US, but still, the FRB was not pressured by the government to rescue it. FRB denied the liquidity support because the directors

1 Muhammad Farooq Arby, "State Bank of Pakistan: Evolution, Functions and Organization" (March 2009) MPRA Paper No. 13614, Accessed: March 03, 2018.

2 Muhammad Mahmood Shah Khan, Bushra Shafiq, and Farrukh Ijaz, "An Empirical Analysis of Banking Sector in Pakistan: Islamic Versus Conventional Banks" (March 2017) *International Journal of Islamic Economics and Finance Studies*, Vol. 3, No. 1, Accessed: October 06, 2018.

of the FRB were of the opinion that, if they injected money into the rescue operation of the concerned bank, it would send the taxpayers' money down the drain.[3] Thus, Pakistan must learn from the examples of the BOE and FRB and erode the unnecessary influence of the politicians from the SBP. The SBP must elucidate its rescue policy for all banking and financial institutions and only lend liquidity when it is in the greater interest of the entire financial system of the state.

## 6.2 Reform Proposals

The SBP is continuously playing the role of LOLR towards many national and private financial institutions by superseding the basic principles of this role. It is commendable that the policymakers of Pakistan recognised the need for a LOLR at the time of the establishment of the CB known as SBP and empowered it to act as a LOLR for the financial institutions which could meet the standards stated in the regulation. However, an express provision regarding the role of LOLR is incorporated through an amendment in 2015, which states overtly the principles which will be followed while acting as LOLR. The first and foremost thing which Pakistan needs to comply with is to understand the acumen of having a LOLR and look at its conception in a wider depiction rather than considering it merely a facility of imparting liquidity in times of emergency. After a deliberate study of the financial systems of the UK and the US and the financial crises of different times, it is identified that a concern among the investors could convert a trivial financial issue into a major financial crisis. Therefore, instead of merely injecting liquidity into the financial institutions or in the financial market, the role of a LOLR is to keep the trust of the depositors. It is argued previously, in the case studies of the UK and USA, that this approach helps to control the demand for liquidity and provides sufficient time to the financial institutions to overcome the liquidity problem.

Notwithstanding, panic among investors drastically increases the demand for liquidity, which compels financial institutions to sell their illiquid assets swiftly. A quick sale of the illiquid assets causes a decrease in their value and leaves no window for the financial institutions but to seek assistance from the CB as a LOLR. In Pakistan, the role of the SBP, particularly in the case of KASB Bank, and an undue influence of politicians are repugnant to the philosophy of having a LOLR. The trust of the creditors is imperative to maintain stability in the financial system. However, the political rhetoric of the failure of the system is spreading panic, which is making it difficult for the SBP to get

3 Gayane Oganesyan, "The Changed Role of LOLR: Crisis Responses of Federal Reserves, European CB and Bank of England" (2013) *Institute for International Political Economy Berlin* 19/2013, Accessed: March 30, 2018.

full benefits from the LOLR facility. Foreign investment helps an economic system to grow, and Pakistan is endeavouring to encourage foreign investors to bring in investment. Nevertheless, for political reasons, government officials may sometimes create panic among existing investors, and this has become somewhat of a political norm to castigate the fiscal policies of the authorities and introduce instability.

Secondly, the SBP must be allowed to work as an independent institution instead of working as a subordinate of government officials. The government's prerogative of appointing the governor of the SBP is a main reason for creating a suspicion of political influence over the institution because, in the presence of a politically appointed head of the institution, there may be less independence of the CB. The governor's selection can be influenced by the directors of the SBP, and final approval can be subject to the advice of the cabinet. Additionally, the SBP role as LOLR, in the case of KASB Bank, lacks the required transparency normally required, for example, with the BOE and FRB. The only requirement is that a factual annual report be presented in parliament stating all the information regarding the operations of SBP as the LOLR.

Thirdly, the principle of charging a high penalty rate on the liquidity support by the CB on LOLR operations is established so that the expenses of such operations can be recovered. However, the SBP failed to recover the original amount imparted as liquidity support. As a result, the SBP started facing liquidity problems and was rescued 18 times by the IMF. Currently, the new government is also striving to get another rescue package from the IMF. The dependency on the support of the IMF will have no end until the system is reformed. The principles of charging a high penalty rate should be followed strictly, with no exceptions. There should be no lending to the financial institutions which are unable to provide collateral. Also, SBP must establish a mechanism to get factual audit reports of the financial institutions working in the system on a regular basis.

Fourthly, the SBP must strictly implement the principle of minimum capital requirement, proposed in the regulation of Basel Accord III for financial institutions, with no exceptions. Besides the requirement of providing worthy collaterals, audit reports of the last five years must be consulted before lending liquidity to a financial institution, which will help to evaluate whether the financial institution is merely facing liquidity challenges or is going to be insolvent. No financial institution must be rescued for the second time without the approval of the cabinet if that institution has failed to repay the amount which was injected for its first rescue. Also, SBP must appoint directors to closely monitor all the financial activities of the institution.

Finally, the problem of having a LOLR facility for Islamic banks based on interest-free liquidity support is also a big challenge for the SBP to address. Islamic banks work as interest-free companies; that is why it is not possible for the SBP to play the role of LOLR for these banks based on the classical theories of LOLR. CBs around the globe charge a high-interest rate to discourage financial institutions from relying on the liquidity support of the LOLR. The SBP, while acting as LOLR for Islamic banks, can use the option of nationalisation, as the BOE did in the case of Northern Rock, because, if liquidity support will be interest-free, it will allow Islamic banks to frequently seek liquidity assistance. Consequently, the SBP will start experiencing a liquidity crisis, which will lead it to seek another bailout package from the IMF. Additionally, the SBP can use the same approach as the Islamic Banks and take a share in the profit of these banks. Furthermore, the SBP can purchase the illiquid shares of Islamic banks instead of directly injecting liquidity into them, and once they overcome the liquidity problem, resell those illiquid assets at market value at a time when SBP can earn as much money as it has spent while playing the role of LOLR. The SBP must impose the condition on Islamic banks that are seeking liquidity support from it that they can only invest in progressive businesses.

### *6.2.1 Implications of Reform Proposals*

It is imperative to reform the functions of the system according to contemporary issues because a rigid approach makes it difficult for the system to address new challenges. Every system is going through a continuous process of evolution, and that is why it is not possible for any system to survive without embedding modern techniques. The system of LOLR existed even before the inception of CBs, and domestic financial institutions borrowed money from banks or other financial institutions when they required it. These borrowings were based on mutual understandings of the parties and were mainly based on personal relations. The countries were also using the same approach at the international level and borrowed money from other countries based on political relations or interests. However, the emergence of banking and economic systems created the need for an official LOLR at domestic and international levels. Therefore, the duty of playing the role of LOLR has played an important part in the inception of the CBs.

The LOLR was badly criticised by most economists because it was merely a duty of the CB to lend liquidity to the financial institutions which were enduring liquidity shortfalls. Moral hazard problems had turned out to be the main cause of the emergence of this role. However, economists like Henry Thornton and Walter Bagehot suggested a framework for the role of LOLR and tried to address the issue of moral hazard problems. Several financial issues have also urged policymakers to recognise the need for this role. Initially, in the UK, it was proposed that the CB would only rescue the financial institutions which could provide good collateral and agreed to pay a high-interest rate on the liquidity support. No financial institution was eligible to seek financial assistance from the CB which was insusceptible to meet the standard of being solvent. Although these suggestions were handy to curtail the anxiety of moral hazard problems, the deliberate examination of the financial crises highlighted many questions on these proposals. It was acknowledged that the assessment of the CB regarding the solvency of the institution during the crisis was wrong, in many cases, and some institutions could be successfully rescued, even if they were unable to provide collateral. Thus, it can be realised that the system was frequently reformed according to the requirements. The BOE used its discretionary powers and lent liquidity to the financial institutions which were unable to provide collateral. In many cases, the interest rate was reduced even from the market rate of the time. All these steps allowed the BOE to perform well during the financial crises, and it had remarkably protected the financial system against crises. Reforms of the system strengthened the system and developed a modern and efficient system; however, if the BOE had continued to act according to the suggestions of Walter Bagehot, it may not have protected the system against crises.[4]

Similarly, in the US, the experiment of the first CB was not successful, but with the passage of time, policymakers have established a system that is now among the best systems in the world. The key to their success was to continuously reform the system and quest for a better one that could address the contemporary issues of that time. The FRB was established in 1913 and mandated to play the role of LOLR for the banking system in the US, which was facing more financial problems than any other banking system of the First World. The powers of the FRB were also subject to the proposal of Walter Bagehot, and it was only providing liquidity support to the banks which were able to provide collateral. However, after the Great Depression (the 1930s), it was recognised that the system related to the LOLR needs to be reformed. The powers of FRB were reformed, and it was authorised to provide liquidity assistance to nonbanks and without strictly imposing the conditions of worthy collateral. The recent financial crisis of 2007–2008 was the biggest test of the capability of the LOLR functions to protect the financial system against crisis. The FRB played the role of LOLR, which was admired by many economists, but it was still reformed through the Dodd-Frank Act, 2010.[5]

In Pakistan, the SBP is authorised to play the role of LOLR for the financial institutions which are working in its jurisdiction. The powers of the SBP are subject to the condition of good collateral. No financial institution can obtain liquidity support from it which is unable to provide collateral. However, this rule is not being followed, and SBP was ordained by the government to lend liquidity to national institutions on several occasions. Non-transparency in the

4 Mike Anson, David Bholat, Miao Kang, and Ryland Thomas, "The Bank of England as LOLR: New Historical Evidence from Daily Transactional Data" (November 2007) Staff Working Paper No. 691, Accessed: March 03, 2018.

5 Paul Tucker, "The LOLR and Modern Central Banking: Principles and Reconstruction" (2014) *Bank for International Settlement*, Page No. 10.

functions of national institutions is one of the main reasons which is causing financial problems in Pakistan. The frequent dependency of financial institutions on the support of the CB has created a situation many times where the economic system of Pakistan was rescued by the IMF. The IMF has imparted liquidity to the SBP 18 times, but still, the financial system of Pakistan is facing uncertainty.[6]

The understanding of the role of LOLR and the realisation of its significance will have a positive effect on the financial system of Pakistan. Due to political milestones, government officials are disseminating information regarding the financial system of Pakistan that it was facing serious financial problems and would require to be rescued by the IMF again. Panic among investors always has adverse effects on the system. Therefore, a policy of not allowing politicians and unprofessional people to talk about the financial conditions for their interests will help the SBP to ensure the trust of the investors in the system. The independence of the SBP will ensure that it can work according to the rules and regulations and will be able to produce positive results. An election among the directors of the concerned bank and the appointment of the governor after the approval of the cabinet will curtail the direct influence of the government on the institutions because, in the past, the governor was appointed based on the personal relations of the politician. Hence, SBP was later used to be governed for personal and political purposes. The independence of the SBP in its functioning and the strict accountability of its employees can bring a revolutionary change in the financial condition of Pakistan.[7]

Furthermore, if the government and the SBP have reached a point where it has become imperative to rescue a national or private financial institution that is not able to provide good collateral and its failure can harm the entire system, the SBP must rescue it but on the conditions of providing an independent audit and feasibility report. It will help the SBP to recognise the problems which are causing financial problems for the institution. All the audit and feasibility reports of the financial institution which are subject to liquidity assistance by the SBP must be produced before the parliament for approval; otherwise, the liquidity support should be denied. It will have a great impact on the financial system of Pakistan and curtail the issues of using the SBP for personal and political purposes. A complete report of the amount which will be used in rescuing the institutions and conditions will become a public document that will decrease embezzlement in the national financial institutions and

6 Ashfaq Ahmad, Muhammad Imran Malik, and Asad Afzal Humayoun, "Banking Developments in Pakistan: A Journey from Conventional to Islamic Banking" (2010) *European Journal of Social Sciences*, Vol. 17, No. 1, Accessed: October 06, 2018.

7 Sara Cheema, "The IMF: Pakistan's History and Future with the LOLR", *Eurasia Review* (June 19, 2017), Accessed: November 04, 2018.

curtail the burden of SBP. It will also discourage financial institutions from depending on the liquidity support of the LOLR.[8]

The Islamic banking sector is swiftly emerging in Pakistan and contributing to the financial growth of the country. Although the starting of the Islamic banking system is good and it is progressing over time, still, the panic of collapse cannot be ruled out. The conventional banks also had a dramatic start, not only in developed countries but in Pakistan as well. A deliberate study of the banking industry and case studies of the collapse of several banks enables policymakers to realise that the banking sector could not survive without having a LOLR. Thus, it is more important to address the issue of which institution would play the role of LOLR for Islamic banks and under which conditions liquidity assistance would be offered. The SBP cannot provide liquidity support to Islamic banks on a high-interest rate, which is a common practice in the operations of LOLR because the working of these banks is interest-free. Therefore, it will enable the SBP to recover its expenses, which will be used in the rescue operation of an Islamic bank if it will take a share of the profits of the bank. Moreover, an assessment of the businesses of these banks will also provide a clear view of which businesses were in loss, and the SBP would be able to impose conditions that those banks could no longer invest in businesses which were in loss. If the issue of LOLR is not addressed for the Islamic banks and is delayed until the collapse of some Islamic banks, it will make it harder for the SBP to maintain stability in the financial system of Pakistan.[9]

## 6.3 Summary, Justification and Concluding Remarks

Lending liquidity to financial institutions is being practised even before the establishment of the CBs. Financial institutions and even natural persons were capable of playing the role of LOLR if they were holding sufficient liquidity which they could lend. There were no laws that could regulate the operations of lending liquidity because these operations were conducted on mutually understood stipulations. Various countries (Germany, Pakistan, KSA) also lent liquidity and rescued the economy of other countries because of their diplomatic relations of political gains. This ritual of lending liquidity at the domestic and international levels has not gone obsolete in the modern economic system. Notwithstanding, CBs at the domestic level and IMF at

8 Ahsin Shahid, Hibba Saeed, and Muhammad Ali Tirmizi, "Economic Development and Banking Sector Growth in Pakistan" (2015) *Journal of Sustainable Finance & Investment*, Vol. 5, No. 3, Accessed: October 07, 2018.

9 Ashfaq Ahmad, Muhammad Imran Malik, and Asad Afzal Humayoun, "Banking Developments in Pakistan: A Journey from Conventional to Islamic Banking" (2010) *European Journal of Social Sciences*, Vol. 17, No. 1, Accessed: October 06, 2018.

the international level are officially playing the role of LOLR. However, the powers of the CBs and IMF to perform the role of LOLR are accountable and regulated by domestic and international regulations. Thus, the CBs and the IMF charge high-interest rates on the liquidity support which they offer while performing the role of LOLR. The support of liquidity also comes only against worthy collateral. A minor liquidity problem can escalate the panic among the creditors and surge the demand for liquidity, which can haul the entire system towards insolvency. More than injecting liquidity into the financial system, the LOLR must assure the trust of the creditors in the system and curtail the demand for liquidity.

This book is divided into six main chapters, and each one of them is segregated further for the better understanding of the reader. The conceptual underpinning of the LOLR and its contemporary significance in the modern financial system is elaborated. The pragmatic experiences of the Bank of England and Federal Reserve are critically examined, and the lessons to reform the current laws of Pakistan are also drawn. In Chapter 1, a comprehensive description of the functions of LOLR and its importance in establishing a stable financial system is provided. Moreover, the progression of LOLR is unfolded, which was considered nothing but lending liquidity to financial institutions during crises. The contributions of Sir Francis Baring, who first used the term LOLR for the CB of the UK, are discussed in detail. The principles of Walter Bagehot and Henry Thornton to address the problem of moral hazard are also briefed. A critical analysis is provided for these principles, which were proposed for the CBs to abide by while playing the role of LOLR. The need for an international LOLR is highlighted, and the emergence of IMF as an official international LOLR is also explained. A continuous dependency of financial institutions on the liquidity support of the CB creates severe moral hazard problems. The causes which enhance the anxiety of moral hazard problems and their solutions are examined in the final part of this chapter.

The banking sector of Pakistan, inception of the Islamic banking and the current position of the recommendations of Basel Accord III are elucidated in third chapter of this book. This chapter was divided into five parts. The banking system which is now a vital part of any financial system and its contributions to the GDP of Pakistan is expressed. The evolution of the banking industry of Pakistan and the impacts of the policies of nationalisation (the 1970s) and privatisation (1990s) on the financial system are examined in detail. Moreover, the inception of a new model of the banking system in the form of Islamic banking (2002) in the system of Pakistan is also discussed. A critical analysis of the factors which cause a financial crisis and the reasons for the instability of the financial system of Pakistan is provided in the second part of this chapter. The third part elaborates the Banking Companies Ordinance, 1962 (LVII of 1962), which regulates the banking sector in Pakistan. The powers and duties of the SBP are also expressed. The fourth part argues the causes which contributed to the collapse of many banks in the world and unfolds the main reasons behind the proposals of the Basel committee. Basel I and II and the reasons for their failure to deter the financial crisis of 2007–2008 are also accessed. The hurdles to implement Basel III are unveiled. Finally, the loopholes in the current regulations which empower the SBP to play the role of LOLR are highlighted, and the challenges of establishing a LOLR for Islamic banking are examined.

Chapter 5 of this book identifies the problem in the regulatory system of Pakistan in the context of LOLR. The chapter also answers the research question of this research. It provides a detailed discussion on the operation of LOLR by the SBP to identify the problem. It argues that the power of acting as LOLR was allocated to the SBP after the financial crisis of 2007–2008. The SBP is empowered to act as LOLR through an amendment in the State Bank of Pakistan Act 1956 in 2015. The section is examined in this chapter. Furthermore, a case study of the KASB Bank is examined to identify the problem. The establishment of the KASB is discussed, besides the functioning of the bank until the merger took place. All of the legal formalities which were required to be fulfilled in the amalgamation of the KASB into the BankIslami are appraised. The chapter concludes by arguing that, although there are loopholes in the regulation, the main problem lies in the transparency issues while conducting LOLR operations.

Chapter 6 provides a detailed assessment of the operations of BOE and FRB as LOLR by evaluating examples. It identifies the gaps of the current system of Pakistan and, after comparing the system of the UK and US, draws lessons to propose a way forward. The establishment of the BOE is discussed, which was established as a commercial bank. Its emergence as a CB for the UK and its rescue operations as a LOLR are also unfolded. The principles of Walter Bagehot and Henry Thornton to curtail the effects of moral hazard problems are described in detail. The use of the discretionary powers while playing the role of LOLR which the BOE keeps is accessed. The establishment of the first CB in the US and the reasons for its collapse are unfolded. The divergence between the first and second CB of the US is also discussed. The era in which the financial system of the US was governed without a CB is evaluated. The establishment of the Federal Reserve and its role in strengthening financial institutions against financial crises is explicated. Dodd-Frank Act, 2010, which regulates the functions of LOLR in the US, is studied. The example of Northern Rock, Lehman Brothers and AIG are accessed to draw lessons for the system of Pakistan. Furthermore, a critical evaluation of the role of LOLR, in the context of the Bank of England, Federal Reserves and State Bank of Pakistan, is provided. The functions and the importance of LOLR in the modern financial system are described. Moreover, the understanding regarding the role of LOLR before the recent financial crisis of 2007–2008 is accessed. The LOLR was limited to lending liquidity to the financial institutions which were facing liquidity problems. The role of the BOE and FRB in protecting financial institutions in the financial crisis of 2007–2008 is explained extensively. The approaches used by the CBs of the UK, US and Pakistan are also expressed in detail. Additionally, the domestic laws which empower the BOE, FRB and SBP are examined. The reasons why policymakers were critical of the role of LOLR for a long time are unfolded.

Chapter 6 unfolds all the changes which were made in the financial laws of the UK and the US to enhance the capacity of the role of LOLR. The BOE possesses several discretionary powers while playing the role of LOLR. However, on the other hand, after the implementation of the Dodd-Frank Act, 2010, the discretionary powers of FRB have been curtailed. Although the SBP is also bound to lend liquidity to the institutions which can provide worthy collateral, it spends a large amount in providing liquidity to rescue national institutions that are not providing any collateral. The loopholes in the current system of Pakistan are identified, and a reform proposal is illustrated. Finally, a critical evaluation of the reform proposal is also provided, which elaborates on the benefits of implementing these reform proposals. The contemporary challenges regarding the LOLR facility for Islamic banking are addressed, and a reform proposal in this regard is provided. The significance of the recommendations of the Basel Accord III in making a stable banking system is also accessed. Furthermore, a summary is provided, besides the justification for undertaking this research. Moreover, the findings of this book are elucidated. Finally, it concludes by providing recommendations for further research and concluding remarks.

### *6.3.1 Findings*

An inevitable need for the LOLR in the modern financial system is established because of its successful operations in rescuing financial institutions during crises. The financial system will be vulnerable and unstable if there are no institutions that can lend liquidity during a crisis. The creditors will also be uncertain about the persistence of the system in the face of financial crises. Although the presence of LOLR addresses all these issues, at the same time, it gives rise to several moral hazard problems. The assurance of the CB to impart liquidity, when it will be needed, erodes the surveillance of the creditors on the activities of the financial institutions because they feel no insecurity for their money. It allows the administration of the financial institutions to invest in risky business ventures without paying heed to the repercussions which can be harmful. The CBs keep the public money, which can also be wasted if it is imparted to financial institutions which are not capable of surviving by utilising their resources. Moreover, the principles of lending freely but to the financial institutions which can provide good collateral and imposition of high-interest rate can be useful to minimise the effects of moral hazard problems (see Chapter 2). Notwithstanding, the main findings which were made through this research are:

a) Moral hazard problems cannot be permanently eliminated but can only be curtailed through the deployment of financial strategies. The fiscal policy of the CB regarding the operations of LOLR should be overtly expressed at the start of each financial year. The CB must not act as a LOLR only during the financial crisis; rather, it must take all necessary steps to prevent a financial crisis. Vigilant financial strategies mean a meticulous assessment of the financial activities of the institutions working within the system quarterly. Assessment includes the maintenance of required liquidity under the Basel Accord, business activities, the risk involved, worth of illiquid assets, etc.
b) The CB must be well informed regarding the strengths and weaknesses of the financial systems. All of the audit reports must be published quarterly. CB must also have a piece of accurate information if the financial institution is merely illiquid or it is facing insolvency challenges.
c) It is not possible to precisely evaluate the difference between illiquidity and insolvency during a financial crisis. Therefore, the CB should make sure that it is having factual reports of the financial institutions working in its domain.
d) No financial system can survive if it fails to ensure impartiality and transparency while playing the role of LOLR. As discussed in Chapter 6, the SBP was not impartial while using its regulatory powers for KASB Bank. Also, the SBP and the government were reluctant to make their report public, which raised serious questions regarding their transparency. Operations of LOLR must be conducted on the approvals of the experts and committees working within the SBP. The Bank of England's example, in the case of Northern Rock, can be followed, in which the government waited for the parliamentary committee's report on "the bank run" before taking any action. To ensure impartiality and transparency in the operations of LOLR, a CB must provide a comprehensive report, which should address the questions of why a LOLR was needed, how it was conducted and why the CB refused to act as LOLR, if applicable. Details of the amount injected and covenants should also be provided, and the CB should make its reports public.
e) The implementation of the proposals of Basel Accord III can make a strong financial system and prevent the collapse of banks (see Chapter 5).

## 6.4 Concluding Remarks

Since the recent financial crisis of 2007–2008, the role of LOLR has been admitted as an inseparable part of the functions of CBs. Although it has demonstrated its role in deterring a financial crisis, the apprehensions of the wastage of public money should not be ruled out. This study has evaluated the role of LOLR played by the BOE and FRB during financial crises and unfolds the fact that it was quite helpful in preventing the collapse of many financial institutions. There is no financial system in which financial institutions do not suffer liquidity challenges, even in developed countries like the UK and the US; the CBs have to impart liquidity to protect their financial institutions. Similarly, it is not astonishing that the financial institutions in Pakistan experience the same, but the reasons for not getting fruitful results through rescue operations are lack of transparency and inefficient laws. Thus, contemporary challenges need to be identified and addressed accordingly.

## 6.5 Summary

This chapter, and indeed, the research more generally, has presented and analysed the problems of the systems of the UK and the US and then explained how the policymakers of both countries have reformed their systems. The book has demonstrated the crucial significance of continuously reforming banking systems and making them efficient to address contemporary issues and concerns. The current financial issues of Pakistan are elucidated and the loopholes in the legislation are examined in the book with a view to looking for precedents to follow in reforming the banking institutions there. Furthermore, reform proposals for the system of Pakistan are proposed to address the gaps in the current regulation and to fully establish a modern banking system. The implications of these reform proposals are examined in detail. The benefits which the financial system of Pakistan can derive from reform are, it is argued, significant, and yet, the repercussions of a lack of reform, in the light and knowledge of what can happen in times of financial crisis, cannot be lightly dismissed.

# Index

Printed in the United States
by Baker & Taylor Publisher Services